vital statistics

Super-rich in carotenes and potassium. *Rich* in vitamin C. *Contains* B vitamins. A Superjuice for mental energy. The red colour in beetroot is similar to that of haemoglobin in blood and is a traditional effective treatment for anaemia, leukaemia and cancer in Eastern Europe. By increasing the oxygen-carrying power of blood, it also increases brain power, concentration and memory.

high flyer

If you've a busy day ahead and little chance of a good meal until the evening, set yourself up with this blood-building, vitamin-laden energy-booster. A massive health-protector and life-extender, the High Flyer should be on everyone's menu at least twice a week. This brain-booster will keep your mental faculties in top gear. As a bonus, it slows skin ageing, prevents sun damage and should be taken regularly before holidays.

spinach 6 leaves
carrots 3, unpeeled; unless organic, remove top and bottom
apple 1, unpeeled, uncored and quartered
beetroot 1 medium, unpeeled, with leaves

the red-eye special

Taken the overnight plane? Been burning the midnight oil? Had a night on the tiles? Whatever the reason, the next day can be hell – but it needn't be. While the Red-eye Special won't work miracles, it comes pretty close. The ingredients in this Superjuice were popular with ancient Greeks and Romans, who knew that the natural oils in parsley and mint soothe the stomach and calm jangley nerves. With clear eyes, no headache and no puffiness or gritty skin, you'll get through the day in better shape than you ever imagined possible.

mint 6 leaves, with sprigs
spinach 6 leaves
melon 1 medium, yellow-fleshed, peeled and deseeded
parsley 1 handful, with stems

vital statistics

Super-rich in potassium and vitamin A. The Red-eye Special is a detoxifying juice, thanks to the parsley in its recipe. Both parsley and mint have a healing effect on the entire digestive system and are calming to the central nervous system. Melon juice also overflows with healing beta-carotenes and is exceptionally curative and cooling. Two or three glasses of this juice will see you through until bedtime – where sleep will add the finishing touches.

peak performer

Never underestimate the power of pears! Few people realise the nutritional value that may be found in a ripe pear of any variety – and the juice adds a unique flavour to this Superjuice. Even just sniffing its wonderful aroma helps set the stage for a real 'feel-good' day. If you're feeling a bit sluggish, then the soluble fibre found in the pears and apples – together with the rich supply of natural sugars in grapes and pineapple – are just the thing to aid digestion and provide instant energy.

grapes 12, black or white
pears 4, unpeeled
apples 2, unpeeled, uncored and quartered
pineapple 2 slices, peeled

vital statistics

Rich in potassium, pectin (soluble fibre) and natural healing enzymes. *Contains* vitamin C, calcium, and traces of B vitamins. In addition to its wealth of vitamins and nutrients, the Peak Performer has other health benefits to offer. The tannins, powerful flavones and other aromatic compounds harboured in grapes combine to make them energising and cancer-fighting – all this in a Superjuice that tastes as great as it smells!

primary pepper punch

A juice to take on a regular basis. Don't be put off if you find green peppers acidic and indigestible: ripe red and yellow peppers are deliciously sweet and succulent. What's more, they combine beautifully with the other vegetables to make this a cocktail with a difference. You'll obtain ultimate antioxidant power from the massive dose of beta-carotenes and other carotenoids that colour these vibrant vegetables.

carrots 2, unpeeled; unless organic, remove top and bottom
beetroot 1 small, unpeeled, with leaves
celery 1 stick, with leaves
yellow pepper ½, deseeded
red pepper ½, deseeded

vital statistics
Super-rich in beta-carotene, vitamins A and C, folic acid and potassium. The iron-rich beet tops help prevent anaemia, so this is a primary Power Juice for women. It's also a real pollution-fighter that declares war on the damaging free radicals present in our environment, so it's especially good for city-dwellers. Of course, there are internal pollutants, too, and if you must smoke, this colourful cocktail will at least give you some increased protection against lung cancer.

pumping iron

Here's a power-pumping iron tonic in a glass for those dull, grey days when you just can't seem to charge up the batteries. It's all too easy to dismiss the cucumber as nothing more than water. While its nutritional content is very low, it is nonetheless regarded as an important healing vegetable in natural medicine – which explains why it appears in lots more recipes. Here, the cucumber's cool, refreshing flavour contrasts superbly with the astringency of beetroot, spinach and watercress.

apples 2, unpeeled, uncored and quartered
beetroot 1 small, unpeeled, with leaves
cucumber 1 medium
spinach 1 handful of leaves
watercress 1 handful

vital statistics

Super-rich in iron, vitamin C and folic acid. *Rich* in beta-carotene and other carotenoids. The vitamin C in this Superjuice makes the iron it contains all the more easily absorbed by the body, while its beta-carotene and other carotenoids protect against cancers. All this, plus its instant supply of natural sugars, makes Pumping Iron the perfect juice for serious exercisers, body-builders, vegetarians and women planning pregnancy.

boxer's beverage

One glass of this Superjuice packs the punch of Mohammed Ali. Overflowing with instantly available essential nutrients, Boxer's Beverage provides power, energy and stamina. The minerals, vitamins and easily utilised calories make this the perfect partner for a high-carbohydrate snack shortly before physical exercise. It's also a great reviver after strenuous exertion.

carrots 4, unpeeled; unless organic, remove top and bottom
kiwi fruit 1, unpeeled
parsley 1 handful with stems
spinach 1 handful of leaves

horse power

It may sound simple, but this classic apple-and-carrot mixture spiked with fresh horseradish is fuel for any bucking bronco. As well as the instant energy derived from the natural sugars in the carrots and apples, the horseradish adds a whole new dimension. You'll get very little juice and lots of pulp from three ounces of horseradish, but what you do get is instant stimulation of the circulation. With the blood coursing through the veins, you'll be ready for anything.

carrots 4, unpeeled; unless organic, remove top and bottom
apples 2, unpeeled, uncored and quartered
horseradish 3 oz fresh

melon and mango tango

Just smelling this wonderful juice first thing in the morning awakens the brain, opens the eyes and quickens the blood. Quick and easy to make, this cool, refreshing drink will kick-start your metabolism and help shrug off that early morning sluggishness. One glass and you'll be running at full power throughout the day.

mango 1, peeled, without stone
melon ½ yellow (cantaloupe, musk or ogen), peeled and deseeded

vital statistics

Super-rich in vitamins A and C. The Melon and Mango Tango provides more than your daily needs of both vitamins listed above. Used for centuries as a diuretic in India, melon helps gets rid of morning puffiness. As a bonus, melons also contain adenosine, a substance that makes blood less sticky, thus reducing the risk of blood clots and heart attack. A super-rich source of instant energy and nutrients, the mango has been cultivated and eaten for more than 4,000 years. The combined vitamin A content of melon and mango juice is a boost to the immune system and helps protect the body from cancer.

spinach spectacular

Spinach Spectacular is the perfect mid-day power booster. Taken with a light lunch, it will see you through a mentally or physically arduous afternoon and still leave you with reserves for an evening on the town. As a bonus, both spinach and watercress contain powerful substances which protect against cancer.

apple 1, unpeeled, uncored and quartered
celery 1 stick, with leaves
spinach 3 oz fresh young leaves
watercress 1 handful

vital statistics

Super-rich in vitamins A, C and folic acid. *Rich* in riboflavin (B$_2$). While a certain sailor-man ate it for iron, spinach is hard to make the most of due to the high levels of oxalic acid in its leaves which stop absorption. Placed in this Superjuice, however, the huge amounts of other vitamins and nutrients it contains would have given Popeye superpowers even he never dreamt of!

green apple power punch

A zappy cleanser to start your day, the Green Apple Power Punch is ideal for stimulating the digestive system and replacing lost minerals following physical activity – on or off the sports field. Take this on an empty stomach and don't eat or drink anything else for half an hour to let its natural fruit sugars do their work.

sorrel 6 leaves
apples 2 large Granny Smith, unpeeled, uncored and quartered
lime 1, peeled (unless key lime)
mint 1 sprig, with stems
parsley 1 handful, with stems

Super-rich in vitamins A, C, E, folic acid and potassium.
Rich in iron and magnesium.
Low in calories, Mediterranean Muscle is a perfect start to the day for weight watchers. It also gets a five-star rating for peak power of mind and body, and is delicious, calming and mildly diuretic to boot. As a final bonus, this Superjuice contains lycopene, one of the most powerful natural antioxidants which protects specifically against heart disease.

mediterranean muscle

Throughout the southern Mediterranean, the combination of tomatoes and basil is inseparable, not only for taste but also for the wonderful mixture of aromas. This Superjuice is another variation on the theme designed for mind and body: it's rich in minerals to give renewed vigour to tired muscles, and contains essential oils from the basil that act specifically on tired minds. Serve with a dash of Worcestershire sauce and some black pepper as a finishing touch.

plum tomatoes 4 large, ripe
carrot 1, unpeeled; unless organic, remove top and bottom
celery 1 stick, with leaves
basil 1 handful
lemon juice of half, squeezed into finished juice

Most of us are familiar with the saying, 'cleanliness is next to godliness'. To the early 20th-century traditional health practitioner, this adage also applied to internal hygiene. Almost a century before 'detox' regimes came into fashion, detoxification was already a key practise of natural medicine.

cleansing

Modern pollution, toxic waste, chemically treated and processed, packaged food make a cleansing regime more vital than ever for good health. By drinking Cleansing Juices, practising simple fasting and avoiding foods that overload the system, you can achieve dramatic results in your overall well-being. Clear eyes and skin, improved digestion, loss of surplus fluid, even a clearer mind... these are just some of the most quickly perceived benefits of inner cleansing. All the juices in this section are designed to improve the efficiency of the body's natural 'housekeeping system'. The recipes use the gentle power of natural foods to stimulate specific organs and functions. The juice of citrus fruits stimulates saliva glands, aiding the digestive process right from its beginnings in the mouth. Herbs and spices increase production of the stomach's digestive juices to ensure the proper breakdown of food and availability of vitamins, minerals and micro-nutrients. Some Cleansing Juices also gently stimulate natural contractions of the bowel, thus

juices

helping to efficiently eliminate waste. Jerusalem artichokes, radishes and dandelions all increase the flow of bile, activate the liver and improve the digestion of fats. In other recipes, celery, parsley, dandelion leaves, lettuce and chicory are used to stimulate the kidneys and deal with fluid retention. Carrots cleanse the skin from the inside outwards. Once you've experienced the feeling of lightness, alertness and inner cleanliness these juices produce, you'll be a firm detox fan. Soon, you'll feel confident enough to tackle the complete 'Detox Juice Diet' on page 152. Whether it's a specific problem such as spots or fluid retention, or just a general bloating, sluggishness or malaise, Cleansing Juices make the ideal rescue remedy.

minty morning

A variation on what has to be the most popular breakfast juice of all.
By combining the health-giving properties of oranges with the natural
oils present in mint (the best digestive of all the herb family), this juice makes a
powerful digestive aid and cleanser that gets to work right from the start.
If you're making this juice in a citrus-fruit juicer (*see* page 154), just halve the
oranges, juice them, chop the mint finely and stir into the juice. If using a regular
juicer, peel the oranges, remove most of the pith and feed small bunches of mint
leaves into the machine between each two or three pieces of orange.

oranges 4 large, peeled, but leaving pith behind
mint a generous sprig, with stems

vital statistics
Super-rich in vitamin C.
Contains potassium, calcium,
folic acid and bioflavonoids.
Oranges boost overall resistance and
are good for the heart and circulatory
system. In natural medicine, they are
also considered beneficial to the
intestines, as they make it difficult
for unwanted bacteria to survive.
They also help with unpleasant problems
such as constipation and wind. Like
most citrus fruits, oranges stimulate
the flow of saliva.

dandelion delight

When Grandma said picking the dandelions would make you wet the bed, she wasn't exactly kidding. Dandelion leaves are a powerful diuretic, and they are hugely popular as a salad vegetable in France, where they are sold as *pis en lit salade*. When combined with the natural fibre in the apple juice and the skin-cleansing properties of carrots, this juice makes a perfect cleanser.

dandelion leaves 6, well-washed (or a handful of parsley if unavailable)
carrots 3, unpeeled; unless organic, remove top and bottom
apples 2, unpeeled, uncored and quartered

vital statistics
Super-rich in vitamin A.
Rich in vitamin C. *Contains* iron.
Definitely not to be taken just before leaving home! The effects of Dandelion Delight may be apparent within half an hour and last for two. All of which makes this is a good Cleansing Juice for women around period time, as it helps eliminate general puffiness and painful, swollen breasts.

vital statistics
Super-rich in vitamins A, C, E and folic acid. *Rich* in potassium and magnesium. Waterfall is a powerful medicine. As well as its strong diuretic effect, it's also a Superjuice that will benefit the skin and is ideal for anyone with high blood pressure or heart disease, since it is very low in sodium. It also makes a safe and excellent Cleansing Juice for use during pregnancy.

waterfall

Another powerful diuretic juice. Waterfall's combination of celery and parsley will help ease even the most stubborn fluid retention. Although English curly parsley is fine for this recipe, the European flat-leafed variety has a richer, fuller and slightly smoother flavour and is, if anything, an even better diuretic.

carrots 3, unpeeled; unless organic, remove top and bottom
apples 2, unpeeled, uncored and quartered
celery 2 sticks, with leaves
parsley 1 handful, with stems

vital statistics

Rich in vitamin C. *Contains* a large amount of soluble fibre in the form of pectin from the apple and pears. The gentle bulking activity of the fibre, combined with the laxative properties of prunes, makes Prune-light Express a good all-round cleanser. Its stimulating effect on the digestive system makes it a gentle laxative, and the vitamin C it contains is always good for the immune system.

prune-light express

Prunes have something of a bad press, but they are a 'natural' natural ingredient to include in any cleansing regime – and they taste terrific. This Superjuice boasts a slightly sweet-and-sour edge and gives off that wonderful aroma of pears. To make it, juice the pears and cooking apple – the sharpness will counteract the sweetness of the prunes. Remove the stones from the prunes and liquefy in a blender with four fluid ounces of water. Add to the juice and stir well.

prunes 4, pitted, soaked overnight in water
pears 2, unpeeled
cooking apple 1 medium, unpeeled, uncored and quartered

women's wonder

When 'that time of the month' rolls around, it's time to down a glassful of this Superjuice. Women's Wonder is a powerful cleanser and, thanks to the fennel, contains phytoestrogens (plant hormones) which help regulate periods and bring some relief from PMS and menopausal symptoms. While this juice has been designed with women in mind, it's fine for men, too!

apples 2, unpeeled, uncored and quartered
carrots 2, unpeeled; unless organic, remove top and bottom
chicory 1 head
fennel ½ bulb

vital statistics

Super-rich in vitamins A and C. Rich in folic acid and potassium. Contains a good amount of iron. The cleansing power of Women's Wonder is due to the influence fennel and chicory exert on liver and kidney functions – perfect for easing the bloating that often accompanies periods. For women going through the menopause, its phytoestrogens act as a natural 'hormone replacement therapy' to help prevent bone loss and subsequent osteoporosis.

jerusalem juice

If you've embarked on a cleansing regime that involves a day or so of restricted food intake and cleansing juices, then this is the Superjuice to start off your morning. Besides its general cleansing properties, it'll keep your blood sugar on an even keel, and the coriander helps suppress the rather flatulent effects produced by the artichokes.

jerusalem artichokes 3, unpeeled, well-scrubbed
carrots 2 unpeeled; unless organic, remove top and bottom
pear 1, unpeeled
coriander 1 handful

vital statistics

Rich in vitamin A. The combined effects of the pectin from the pear, the inulin from the artichokes and the cleansing aromatic oils from the coriander make this a real powerhouse of a Cleansing Juice. Jerusalem artichokes are the richest source of inulin: a type of sugar. While inulin is not converted into energy, it is a great stimulant of the immune system – a valuable asset while detoxing.

watermelon man

Naturopaths regard melon as a cooling cleanser, and in Indian Ayurvedic medicine it's used as an effective diuretic. It is also cooling to the body and soothing to the digestion. The addition of watercress, broccoli and the tart cooking apple make this 'green juice' a perfect cleanser for men, because it has a testosterone-enhancing effect. It's gently laxative and a powerful immune booster.

cooking apple 1, unpeeled, uncored and quartered
green melon ½ peeled and deseeded
broccoli florets 3 oz, without thick stems
watercress 1 handful

vital statistics
Rich in vitamins A, C and E. *Contains* folic acid, magnesium and potassium. This juice is particularly suitable for physically active men who enjoy regular sport (of course, women can take it, too). The mineral content will also replace losses experienced through sweating. As a regular cleansing juice taken once or twice weekly, the watercress and broccoli ensure a substantial intake of cancer-fighting nutrients.

rainbow cocktail

This mixture of orange, pink, green and yellow-skinned citrus fruits is both a liver and intestinal cleanser. Its clean, tangy, wide-awake taste also makes it a favourite anytime drink. Use the Rainbow as an excellent start to the detox cleansing day. And if you are unfortunate enough to wake up with a hangover, then this cocktail works better than the hair of any dog!

oranges 2, peeled, but leaving pith
lemon 1, with peel if thin-skinned
lime 1, peeled (unless key lime)
***pink grapefruit** 1, peeled, leaving pith behind

If taking prescribed medicines, consult your doctor before drinking large amounts of grapefruit juice

vital statistics

Super-rich in vitamin C. *Rich* in vitamin A. *Contains* a useful amount of potassium and calcium.
The acidity of all these citrus-fruit juices helps remove some of the unwanted bacteria from the digestive tract and encourages the growth of beneficial probiotic bacteria. Besides tasting terrific, the Rainbow Cocktail is a real digestive aid, which should be drunk for two or three days after a course of antibiotics to get your system back in good running order as soon as possible.

vital statistics

Rich in **vitamin C**, **soluble fibre** and **natural sugars**. *Contains* **antioxidant bioflavonoids** and **potassium**. The pith of lemons is rich in a natural substance called **limonene**, now believed to have anti-cancer properties. For this reason, when making the Lemon Express, it's best to peel the lemon first, leaving on the white pith and then put it through your juicer, rather than using a citrus-fruit juicer which leaves all the helpful pith behind.

lemon express

Grapes are one of Nature's great cleansers. Because of their high natural sugar content, they should always feature in any detox regime. If you're cleansing your digestive system and reducing food consumption, the extra sugar will keep your energy levels up. The combination of grapes, soluble fibre in the apples and the gentle diuretic effect of the lemon makes this juice particularly effective.

apples 3, unpeeled, uncored and quartered
lemon 1, with peel if thin-skinned
white grapes 4 oz

vital statistics

Super-rich in vitamins A, C and E. *Rich* in folic acid and potassium. *Contains* useful amounts of some B vitamins. The legendary diuretic powers of parsley stimulate the kidneys, while the fibre from the carrots and red pepper stimulate the normal contractions of the large bowel, hastening elimination. The combined blood-purifying benefits of beetroot and spinach add the final touch to this superb Cleansing Juice, which also replenishes the body's stores of essential nutrients.

pepper purifier

In need of a powerful Superjuice to purify the system? Then look no further than the Pepper Purifier – a particularly important juice to be used after periods of illness that necessitate medication. Taken on alternate days for a week, it will help the body dispose of any drug residues.

carrots 3, unpeeled; unless organic, remove top and bottom
beetroot 1 small, unpeeled, with leaves
red pepper ½, deseeded
parsley 1 handful, with stems
spinach 1 handful of leaves

ginger spice

Ginger Spice is a gentle cleanser which benefits from the powerful volatile oils zingiberene and gingerol present in the ginger, as well as the cleansing and digestive benefits of carrot, apple and orange. This Cleansing Juice has powerful antiseptic and anti-inflammatory benefits and is perfect to use at the onset of a cold or fever, or immediately after a bout of food poisoning.

carrots 2, unpeeled; unless organic, remove top and bottom
apple 1, unpeeled, uncored and quartered
orange 1, peeled, leaving pith behind
ginger 1 oz, peeled and sliced

vital statistics
Rich in vitamins A, C and fibre. Ginger is one of the most versatile and valuable of spices. The ancient Greeks used it for digestive problems and as an antidote to poisoning, while medieval herbalists valued its warming properties highly. In the many ginger recipes you'll find in this book, it also provides an invigorating lift – particularly in the 'Aphrodisiac Juice' chapter!

radish revolution

The radish is a much overlooked and highly valuable vegetable – so valuable, in fact, that the ancient pharaohs used them (along with garlic and onions) to pay the workers who built the pyramids! A member of the cabbage family, radishes also contain anti-cancer nutrients. Combined with the diuretic power of dandelion (or parsley) and the cleansing benefits of carrots, this sharp, peppery juice will revolutionise your cleansing programme.

carrots 6, unpeeled; unless organic, remove top and bottom
dandelion leaves 6, well-washed (or a handful of parsley if these are unavailable)
radishes 4 medium-sized

vital statistics

Rich in vitamin A, potassium and sulphur. *Contains* some vitamin C and selenium.
As part of this Cleansing Juice, radishes stimulate the gall bladder to increase the release of bile, as well as stimulating the liver. These properties combine to make Radish Revolution a real fat-buster – a Superjuice not to be missed from any detox programme.

vital statistics

Rich in vitamins A and C, potassium, and pectin. It is the volatile oils of anisic acid, fenchone and anethole that give fennel its unique flavour as well as its diuretic, cleansing and digestive properties. Although fennel itself isn't bursting with nutrients, it more than makes up for this deficiency with its role as a potent purifier.

the florentine

Although Florence fennel (to give it its full name) has been grown for more than 2,000 years, it is more commonly used in England for its pale green fronds which go so well with fish. Yet with its unique taste and aroma of aniseed, the fennel bulb is also a gentle diuretic and digestive aid. Combined here with the sweeter carrot and fruit flavours, it makes a delicious and therapeutic mixture.

apples 2, unpeeled, uncored and quartered
pears 2, unpeeled
carrot 1, unpeeled; unless organic, remove top and bottom
fennel 1 medium bulb

Super-rich in vitamin A and carotenoids. *Rich* in potassium, folic acid. *Contains* useful amounts of vitamin C, B vitamins, iron and iodine.

The antiseptic and antifungal sulphur compounds in the chives, the diuretic and calming oils in lettuce and the unique digestion-promoting constituents of coriander make Quartet in 'C' a highly potent mixture – the perfect 'note' on which to end this Cleansing Juices chapter!

quartet in 'c'

The calorie-conscious know that lettuce is 95 per cent water and has hardly any calories – yet its nutritional value is enough to surprise anyone. It harbours some vitamin C, beta-carotene, calcium, potassium, a little iodine, a little iron and substantial amounts of folic acid. Since it is also cleansing, cooling and mildly diuretic, lettuce makes this a special Cleansing Juice that is an ideal tonic for the digestive system, eyes and skin.

carrots 3, unpeeled; unless organic, remove top and bottom
cos lettuce 1 (smallish)
coriander 1 small bunch
chives 1 small bunch

Almost two centuries ago, the doctrine of vitalism held that the origin and phenomena of life are the result of a vital principle – not just of purely chemical or physical forces. Vitality is that force: the captive dynamic power present in seeds, nuts, berries, fruits and vegetables.

vitality

Because they harness the forces of sunlight, earth and water, these growing things contain everything we need to live life to the full. To be healthy, active and mentally alert; to produce fine, strong children; to avoid the diseases of the modern world and unnecessary ill health in old age... all this and more is within everyone's grasp.

Designed as it is, the human body should survive in an active, healthy state for as much as 120 years. So why doesn't it? Part of the answer lies in the modern, hectic world we live in. Increased stress levels, sedentary jobs and greater pollution are all factors, but – more importantly – so is our diet. By moving away from natural foods with their inherent vitality, we have sold ourselves short. We may well be living longer than our ancestors, but we're having to deal with such diseases as cancer and chronic fatigue syndrome, CJD and Alzheimer's disease, arthritis and Parkinson's disease. I can't guarantee that you will avoid all these, but if you

juices

want to give the scales a massive tilt in your favour, then look no further than Vitality Juices.

These juices contain powerful antioxidant nutrients that neutralise dangerous free radicals. Some are laden with carotenoids that protect the eyes. Some are simply bursting with vitamin E, which promotes fertility. Others are rich in substances that protect against a wide variety of cancers. Does juicing really promote vitality? Well, a sprightly patient told me on his 90th birthday that he still had two ambitions in life. One was to get a centenary telegram from the Queen; the other was to be shot by a jealous husband. He has been Vitality Juicing for 50 years – so I'm not sure he was joking!

apple and watercress energiser

This is the ultimate vitality Superjuice, ideal as a regular booster once or twice a week, and essential at times of greater stress, increased workload or any time when your body and mind need to be bursting with vitality and creative energy. It also promotes greater concentration and is an aid to mental agility and physical activity – which is precisely why it's called the 'Energiser'.

apples 2, unpeeled, uncored and quartered
carrots 2 large, unpeeled; unless organic, remove top and bottom
tomatoes 2 medium
kiwi fruit 1, unpeeled
watercress 1 handful
spinach 1 handful of leaves

vital statistics

Super-rich in vitamin C. *Rich* in vitamin A, beta-carotene, potassium, magnesium and zinc. *Contains* iron, calcium, and lycopene. Because of its high vitamin C content – more, in fact, than your minimum daily requirement – the Apple and Watercress Energiser will help ward off many a common cold or bout of the 'flu. Its lycopene guards against heart disease and cancer – not bad for something that is also a terrific booster-juice!

blue passion

Here's a juice that is guaranteed to chase away the blues, put a glow on the skin and keep you super-active. It looks good, tastes good and does you good because it overflows with masses of nutrients. Blue Passion is a real tonic: just one glass will give you instant energy and high levels of immunity. What better way to start the day?

passion-fruit 3, flesh scooped out into juicer
cantaloupe melon 1 medium, peeled
mango 1, peeled, without stone
blueberries 4 oz

vital statistics

Super-rich in vitamin A and C. *Rich* in carotenoids. *Contains* B vitamins and vitamin E, potassium and some calcium. The abundant carotenoids are Blue Passion's most important asset: they're hugely protective against degenerative diseases and cancers, as well as being just plain good for your eyes. This magical mixture is better than turning water into wine or lead into gold. Pity the alchemists never stumbled on this formula...

Super-rich in vitamin C, beta-carotene, and a range of other carotenoids. *Rich* in vitamins A and E. *Contains* folic acid, potassium and immune-boosting phytochemicals.

The combined benefits of Power Pack make it a real stress-buster. The acids in apples break down fatty foods, while the huge amounts of carotenoids in kiwi fruit are protective and energy-enhancing. Celery adds a calming effect, helping to eliminate stress and keeping blood pressure low; no wonder Hippocrates used it around 2,000 years ago for this very reason!

power pack

Pears, apples, celery, kiwi fruit: you'll search hard to find a juice that packs a more powerful punch in the vitality stakes than Power Pack. Never ignore the nutritional value of pears: they're much more than just a sweet fruit. Like apples, they're rich in pectin, easily digested and help the body eliminate cholesterol – all of which make this a highly valuable Vitality Juice.

apples 2, unpeeled, uncored and quartered
kiwi fruit 2, unpeeled
pears 2, unpeeled
celery 1 stick, with leaves

Super-rich in **vitamins A, C**, and **carotenoids**. The Tropical Revitaliser provides specific anti-cancer, antiviral and anti-bacterial substances which have a direct effect on the immune system. The healing enzymes in pineapple also make this a valuable Superjuice to take after physical activity, injury or surgery. And what better way to recharge the batteries on a hot summer's evening than with a glassful of something this fabulous?

tropical revitaliser

It may be summertime, but in the city, the living ain't easy. With massive amounts of pollution-borne free radicals, bacteria and viruses pumping through air-conditioning systems, the office is a particularly dangerous place. But fear not! This Superjuice will boost your natural resistance and revitalise your energy levels. What's more, it tastes great: the sharp cooking apple contrasts with the sweetness of pineapple and mango, all of which blend beautifully with the berry flavours.

cooking apple 1 Bramley, unpeeled, uncored and quartered
mango 1, peeled, without stone
pineapple ½, unpeeled
blueberries 4 oz
strawberries 4 oz

tutti-frutti

It's no coincidence that grapes are one of the most popular fruits given to sick or convalescing people. They're uniquely nourishing, regenerating and strengthening. When combined with the protective constituents of peaches, kiwi fruit and strawberries – not to mention the extraordinary antioxidant powers of passion-fruit and pomegranate – grapes make this is one of the most powerful of all Vitality Juices.

strawberries 6 medium
kiwi fruit 2, unpeeled
passion-fruit 2, flesh scooped out into juicer
peaches 2, stoned
pomegranate 1, seeds and flesh scooped into juicer
red grapes 6 oz

vital statistics
Rich in vitamins A and C. Although rich in vitamins, this Superjuice is far more valuable for the tannins, flavones, enzymes and other essential aromatic oils it provides. Just one glass of Tutti-Frutti contains the quintessential vitality-enhancing and life-protecting elements of Nature. So what are you waiting for? Down the hatch!

in the pink

The colloquial saying 'in the pink' means to be in very good health – and that's what this juice will help you to be. In the West, plums are not usually thought of as being particularly health-giving, but Oriental medicine knows better. This simple, quick and delicious juice is an instant shot in the arm that's rich in blood-building vitality-boosters.

red plums 6, stoned
red apples 2, unpeeled, uncored and quartered
*pink grapefruit 2, peeled, leaving pith behind
*If taking prescribed medicines, consult your doctor before drinking large amounts of grapefruit juice

vital statistics
Super-rich in vitamin C and bioflavonoids. *Rich* in potassium and carotenes. Thanks to the plums, In the Pink is also a valuable source of iron which can be easily absorbed due to its high vitamin C content. Make sure you peel the grapefruit carefully before juicing, however, leaving behind as much pith as possible to preserve the vitality-enhancing bioflavonoids and pectin.

apple tart

Here's an eye-opening vitality juice to start your day. The sweetness of the apples and the sharp acidity of the lemon juice cleanse the palate, while the volatile esters provide a head-clearing aroma that will get anyone off to a good start. Experiment with different varieties and mixtures of apples. For this juice, the most aromatic will produce the greatest benefits.

apples 4, unpeeled, uncored and quartered
lemon 1, with peel if thin-skinned

vital statistics

Super-rich in vitamin C. *Contains* bioflavonoids and limonene. 'An apple a day keeps the doctor away,' says the proverb – and it's almost true. The special soluble fibre in apples helps the body eliminate cholesterol, and eating two a day is enough to make a measurable difference in a short space of time. Even smelling the aroma of fresh apples is enough to lower your blood pressure, and it can sometimes prevent the onset of a migraine attack.

wrinkle zapper

Yes, I know. It's a pain taking the stones out of all those cherries, but it's well worth it: you end up with the most delicious juice you've ever tasted. Do make sure you choose dessert cherries rather than the cooking variety, however, which are very sour. Buy the darkest-coloured ones you can find, as they're the richest in the highly protective natural substances that make this such a valuable Vitality Juice.

apples 2, unpeeled, uncored and quartered
cherries 12 oz, stoned

vital statistics
Super-rich in vitamin C. *Rich* in carotenoids. *Contains* folic acid and potassium. The real bonus of this juice is its huge concentration of substances called anthocyanidins and proanthocyanidins which, among other things, have powerful protective and regenerative properties directly linked to collagen. You won't need those injections if you consume regular amounts of the Wrinkle Zapper – a much safer and cheaper alternative!

athlete's pit-stop

This Vitality Juice is really the 'Wrinkle Zapper Mark II', but our American cousins will grasp the significance of this juice's name, since they call cherry stones 'pits'. Like the Wrinkle Zapper, Athlete's Pit-stop is full of collagen-protecting substances that make this a boon for the regular athlete or exerciser, since collagen forms the building blocks of the cartilage, ligaments and tendons that are so prone to damage during sport.

apple 1, unpeeled, uncored and quartered
pear 1, unpeeled
cherries 12 oz, stoned

strawberry fayre

This juice is best made when strawberries are in season, since that's when they have their highest nutrient content. Pick your own or buy locally grown varieties whenever possible, as these delicate fruits don't travel well. Often thought of as too acidic and bad for arthritics, the truth is the exact opposite. Combined with the pear, peach and lemon, this is a 100-octane Vitality Juice.

peach 1, stoned
pear 1, unpeeled
lemon ½, with peel if thin-skinned
strawberries 16 oz

scarborough fair

Just like the traditional folk-song made famous by Simon and Garfunkle, this juice is the ideal combination of vital force and calming influences. It's the gentle giant of Vitality Juices, since it nourishes body, mind and spirit. As a bonus, it also enhances memory, is cleansing and – thanks to the sage and thyme – is mildly antiseptic.

sage 6 leaves
carrots 4, unpeeled; unless organic, remove top and bottom
celery 3 sticks, with leaves
thyme 1 small sprig (place leaves only into juicer)
parsley 1 handful, with stalks
rosemary 2 teaspoons, removed from stalks

vital statistics

Super-rich in vitamin A and carotenoids. *Rich* in vitamin C and folic acid. *Contains* potassium, calcium and small amounts of other B vitamins. The natural diuretic properties of celery and parsley give Scarborough Fair its cleansing properties, while the sage stimulates liver function, the rosemary improves memory and concentration and the thyme is a good antiseptic. This is an ideal choice for those dark, autumn and winter mornings when you need help in getting both body and mind into gear.

pawpaw punch

It doesn't matter how good the food is that you eat; if it's not digested properly, it's of little benefit – a fact that Shakespeare, with his extraordinary perceptions of the human body and its frailties, knew only too well. 'Now, good digestion,' says Macbeth in 'The Scottish Play', 'wait on appetite, and health to both.' The Bard would never have sampled a pawpaw, but he certainly would have approved of this Vitality Juice, which is both a stimulant of appetite and improver of digestion.

pawpaws 2 large, deseeded, flesh scooped out of skin)
cantaloupe melon ½, peeled
lime ½, peeled (unless key lime)
grapes a small bunch

vital statistics
Super-rich in vitamins A and C and beta-carotene. *Rich* in potassium. *Contains* papain, a powerful, protein-digesting enzyme that is especially effective on all meats. The tannins in the grape skins are an appetite stimulant, while cantaloupe is surprisingly rich in nutrients but also contains digestive enzymes. This combination generates maximum vitality through optimum digestion.

kohl slaw

Kohlrabi is a direct descendant of the ancient wild cabbage introduced to Germany from Italy during the Middle Ages. Sadly, its popularity has not spread far beyond its German borders, but this ugly-looking bulbous vegetable tastes like a mixture of turnips and cabbage with a dash of peppery radish thrown in. As a founder member of the brassica vegetables – along with cabbage, cauliflower, broccoli, Brussels sprouts and many others – it's a powerful booster of the immune system and protects against many forms of cancer.

carrots 3, unpeeled; unless organic, remove top and bottom
celery 1 stick, with leaves
kohlrabi 1 small (bulb and leaves)
fennel ½ bulb

vital statistics

Super-rich in vitamins A, C and E.
Rich in vitamin B$_6$, folic acid
and potassium. *Contains* iron,
calcium and magnesium.
In traditional medicine, beetroot has
long been regarded as a blood improver –
with good reason, considering all the
nutrients and vitamins it contains.
That is precisely why, in Eastern Europe,
beetroot juice is still used as part of
the treatment for leukaemia.

beet treat

Vitality depends on every cell in the body receiving its fair share of good
nutrition. The only way this can happen is when nutrients are absorbed by the
blood and carried throughout the circulatory system, where essential nutrients
are made available to individual cells. If your blood is not in peak condition,
it won't perform this function efficiently, and vitality flags. This Vitality Juice
helps build better blood and provides essential ingredients for cell protection.

carrots 3, unpeeled; unless organic, remove top and bottom
apples 2, unpeeled, uncored and quartered
beetroot 1 small, unpeeled, with leaves

vital statistics

Super-rich in vitamin A and carotenoids. *Rich* in sulphur and vitamin C. The Spring Clean Tonic is more important for its phytochemicals rather than for its basic vitamins and minerals. Special carotenoids in spinach and spring greens protect the eyes against degenerative diseases and the extra beta-carotenes from red pepper and cucumber help revitalise skin and the mucous membranes of the nose and throat. A great boost for the immune system, this tonic raises your vitality quotient in time for spring.

spring clean tonic

After a long, hard winter of cold weather, dull days and dark mornings and evenings, vitality can reach its lowest ebb. If you haven't boosted yours with fresh juices, then now's the time to start. Decoke your sluggish system with this blood-purifying, body-cleansing and vitality-stimulating drink. Honestly, it tastes much better than it sounds!

carrots 3, unpeeled; unless organic, remove top and bottom
spring greens 1 large leaf
cucumber ½ medium
red pepper ¼ deseeded
watercress 1 generous handful
spinach 1 generous handful of leaves

vital statistics

Super-rich in beta-carotene and carotenoids. *Rich in* vitamin C, riboflavin and folic acid. *Contains* potassium and phosphorus. As well as the nutritional benefits listed above, the Octet con Spirito offers a host of other health benefits. The natural substances in garlic lower cholesterol and are also antibacterial and antifungal. Asparagus is cleansing and diuretic, while spring onions and garlic both help ward off chest infections.

octet con spirito

Introducing the ultimate Vitality Juice. These eight vegetables combine to boost immunity, stimulate the liver, activate the kidneys and build better blood. The Octet con Spirito also reduces blood pressure, lessens the likelihood of blood clots and revitalises the libido. And you don't even have to recycle a can once you've drunk it down!

asparagus 3 spears
carrots 3 large, unpeeled; unless organic, remove top and bottom
radishes 3, with leaves
celery 2 sticks, with leaves
beetroot 1 small, unpeeled, with leaves
garlic 1 clove, peeled
spinach 1 handful of leaves
spring onion 1 medium

'Properly speaking, there are no aphrodisiacs capable of endowing those blind to life with sight,' said Napoleon's chef, Kurmonsky. 'But for those with poor eyesight in this matter, there are substances which can act as magnifying lenses.' Folklore is full of magic foods said to awaken that

aphrodisiac

slumbering Greek goddess of love and beauty, Aphrodite. But is there any truth in these old wives' (or husbands') tales? Surprisingly, many of the traditional aphrodisiac foods are indeed rich in nutrients that are vital to sexual performance and fertility. Oysters, for example, are the great traditional aphrodisiac food for men; Casanova reputedly ate 70 a day! Yet while they are extremely rich in zinc, which is essential for sperm formation, they don't happen to juice too well. So eat your oysters (or feed them to the man in your life) in the usual way, but instead of washing them down with Champagne or other forms of alcohol, try any one of these delicious Aphrodisiac Juices. The nuts and seeds they contain are useful for zinc and selenium; asparagus for its vitamins A and E; wheat germ, bananas and avocados for vitamins B and E. The heady aroma of volatile oils in rosemary can jump-start the senses in many ways – as can the stimulating effects of hot spices. Amazing substances in chocolate

juices

do in fact generate feelings of euphoria – similar to the feelings experienced while being in love. These foods work equally well for women and men.

I don't guarantee that the juices in this chapter are the equivalent of Viagra™ in a glass, but their ingredients have a centuries-old aphrodisiac reputation and they certainly don't harbour any unwanted side-effects. Most of them are quick and easy to make, and all are delicious. Some recipes need a combination of juicing and blending. If you don't have a blender, you can use one of the hand-held 'wand' type processors, or (for most recipes) a whisk is almost as good. So if you want to give your romance an added edge, get juicing, and may Cupid watch over you!

ginger up juice

Ginger is a vital ingredient in ancient Chinese medicine and the traditional Ayurvedic healing of India. As well as its powerful medicinal actions, ginger is immensely stimulating. When we use the expression 'ginger someone up', we're invoking the genuine properties of this wonderful root. Combined with the cooling, energising properties of watermelon, this is one of the simplest yet most effective Aphrodisiac Juices.

ginger 1 oz fresh root
watermelon ¼ large, with seeds and skin

vital statistics

Contains small amounts of **vitamins A, C** and **E**. Ginger Up Juice is not included in this book purely for its nutritional value. It does contain traces of vitamins, but these are not significant; its enzymes and gentle diuretic substances are its true assets. Ginger contains substances called **gingerol** and **zingiberene**, which dilate the blood vessels and improve circulation – vital for male sexual performance, but equally important for female enjoyment.

sweet surrender

Bananas are credited with aphrodisiac powers in the folklore of many countries, but don't eat them until they're fully ripe – *ie*, when the skins are completely yellow and starting to mottle with brown specks. In Asia and the Middle East, honey is regarded as a great aphrodisiac. This delicious and refreshing smoothie combines all the enzyme and energising benefits of watermelon with the staying power of bananas. To make it, juice the watermelon, then combine with ice-cubes, honey, yoghurt and banana in a blender.

banana 1, peeled
live yoghurt 1 carton, plain
watermelon ¼, with seeds and skin; cut to fit juicer
honey 1 teaspoon
ice-cubes 1 handful

vital statistics

Rich in calcium, potassium, vitamins A, C and E, and chromium. The potassium in bananas is great for lovers, since it fosters prolonged muscular effort without cramp. Bananas are also one of the very few fruits containing chromium, a mineral essential for energy metabolism and sexual function. The instant energy from the honey and banana will give your love-life a helpful kick-start, too!

Super-rich in vitamin C. *Rich* in potassium. Full of healing and stimulating enzymes, Oriental Magic gets its punch from the volatile oils of ginger and the flavonoids, cumarins and other plant chemicals found in coriander. The contrasting flavours of pineapple and ginger, together with the powerful phytochemicals present in coriander, give this juice a surprising but nonetheless delicious flavour.

oriental magic

The aphrodisiac properties of ginger (*see* page 62) are reinforced in this recipe by coriander, one of the most ancient culinary and medicinal plants. Over the past 3,500 years, its use has spread from ancient Egypt and China, through Asia, North Africa and into Europe, where it has been used as an aphrodisiac since the Middle Ages. A candle-lit supper, a smouldering incense stick, a glass of Oriental Magic and a rug in front of the fire... well, need I say more?

pineapple ½, with skin; cut to fit juicer
ginger ½ oz fresh root
coriander 1 small bunch

Rich in **vitamins** A and C.
Contains some B **vitamins**,
folic acid and **potassium**.
The plant chemicals in pumpkin have a
gentle aphrodisiac effect, but it's the
capsaicin in the chilli pepper that is a
remarkable circulatory stimulant. It has
a dramatic effect on blood flow and male
potency. A glass at bedtime should
almost guarantee a hot and juicy night.

hot and juicy

In the traditional Ayurvedic medicine of India – home of the fabled *Kama Sutra* – the pumpkin is believed to both preserve and increase male virility. In Hot and Juicy, its cool, health-giving juice is combined deliciously with the distinctive flavour of apple and the unusual, slightly nutty taste of lamb's lettuce. The sting in the tail comes from the red chilli – so be prepared for fireworks!

apple 1, unpeeled, uncored and quartered
pumpkin 12 oz, peeled
red chilli ½ small, deseeded
lamb's lettuce 1 handful

femme fatale

Unless you have North African or Arabic friends, or have travelled to these parts of the world, you may never have heard of, let alone tasted, purslane. But it has been used as a medicinal plant since Roman times, and eaten as a vegetable long before that. It's one of the few plant sources of omega-3 fatty acids – and these are the ingredients that make it a mood-enhancing food for women. You should be able to find it in ethnic shops which stock African or Moroccan foods.

sweet apples 4, unpeeled, uncored and quartered
radishes 4 medium
purslane 8 oz
alfalfa sprouts 1 handful

vital statistics

Rich in vitamins A and C. *Contains* some calcium and B vitamins. Femme Fatale gets a hefty shot of phytoestrogens from the radishes, sensuous volatile oils from apples and calming B vitamins from alfalfa sprouts. Add the essential fatty acids and bladder-calming substances derived from the purslane, and this is just the juice to trigger a fatal attraction.

eastern promise

This most potent of Aphrodisiac Juices has a history shrouded in the mists of time. The sacred fig tree of India has been worshipped for 5,000 years, and the Spartan athletes of ancient Greece were fed a diet rich in figs to improve their performance – and not just in the arena. Add the noblest of fruits (the grape), which is cooling and aphrodisiac in itself, plus the oriental aroma of pawpaw, and you truly have an Aphrodisiac Juice that is filled with Eastern Promise.

fresh figs 2, large
pawpaw 1, deseeded, flesh scooped out of skin
black grapes 8 oz

vital statistics

Super-rich in **vitamins** A and C.
All three ingredients in Eastern Promise are bursting with volatile oils and hormone-stimulating properties. The high quantity of fruit sugars in this juice provide instant energy, while the digestion-improving enzymes from the pawpaw make it the ideal accompaniment to a meal when your planned dessert is, shall we say, more interesting than ice-cream.

cherry ripe

Don't be fooled by the seemingly innocent ingredients in Cherry Ripe:
its effects can be powerful and rapid. The sensuous aroma of strawberries,
combined with the sweet, heady taste of cherry juice, makes this simple
recipe extra special. As a bonus, the natural aspirin-like substances found
in strawberries make Cherry Ripe a particularly good juice for anyone
with unwanted aches and pains who's planning a night of passion.

strawberries 16 oz, topped
cherries 8 oz, stoned

vital statistics

Super-rich in vitamin C. *Rich* in bioflavonoids and vitamin A. *Contains* calcium, potassium, folic acid, B vitamins and some magnesium. In addition to stimulating the senses, this Aphrodisiac Juice helps neutralise uric acid – that is why it's so helpful for those with rheumatism, arthritis or even gout. The volatile oils produce a heady perfume that is at once sensuous and arousing – which makes removing all those cherry stones well worth the effort!

french kicker

Garlic as an aphrodisiac? *Mai, oui!* After all, 50 million Frenchmen can't be wrong! Combined with a selection of colourful salad leaves (make sure you add plenty of the darker-coloured and red ones), this juice is both a sexual stimulant and has a calming effect on the mind. Hence, it takes away all those anxieties that so commonly lead to poor performance.

carrots 2, unpeeled; unless organic, remove top and bottom
garlic 1 clove, peeled
lime 1, with peel
salad leaves 12 oz, mixed

vital statistics

Rich in vitamins A, C and E. *Contains* chlorophyll, magnesium, potassium and silicon. As a bonus, the French Kicker is a really good hair tonic – but you're not thinking about that now! Just enjoy the calming natural opiates in the lettuce, the stimulating sulphur compounds in the garlic and the bioflavonoids in the lime that strengthen the circulatory system. It's enough to make anyone say *ooh la la!*

passionate pumpkin

It's the tiny pinch of saffron that adds the vibrant colour tones to this already bright-yellow juice. Certainly the most expensive spice in the world – it takes more than 20,000 hand-picked stigmas and styles from the saffron crocus to make four ounces – saffron is also highly prized for its aphrodisiac properties. Used in ancient India, Greece and Rome, it was also reputed by medieval herbalists to quicken the spirit and heart. To make this delectable concoction, juice the pumpkin, mango and apricots then liquidize with the other ingredients.

apricots 2, stoned
mango 1, peeled and stoned
pumpkin 1 slice, peeled

then blend with:
wheat germ 1 dessert spoon
sesame seeds 1 teaspoon
saffron 1 tiny pinch
ice-cubes 1 handful

vital statistics
Super-rich in vitamins A, C and carotenoids. *Rich* in vitamin E, B vitamins and zinc. Passionate Pumpkin makes a potent remedy for both sexes which also encourages the production of healthy sperm; what's more, it makes a perfect drink at any time of the day. The volatile constituents from saffron also help soothe menstrual cramps and pain.

mountain rescue

Swiss chard may seem an unlikely contender to include in an Aphrodisiac Juice, but it's rich in nutrients and you can juice the leaf as well as the fleshy stalk. In case you feel like serenading your partner, leeks are good for the voice – the Roman emperor Nero ate some every day to improve his – but they're also a soothing nerve tonic.

swiss chard 4 leaves
leek 3 inches
apples 3, unpeeled, uncored and quartered
asparagus 2 spears
celery 2 sticks, with leaves

vital statistics

Super-rich in vitamins A, C and folic acid. *Rich* in carotenoids and potassium. *Contains* iron and some vitamin E. Mountain Rescue is a valuable aphrodisiac tonic for late-summer/early autumn – an ideal way to get ready for those long, snowy winters! The folic acid and vitamin E it contains provide vital stimulants, while the sulphur compounds in leeks help reduce cholesterol and improve blood flow.

bunnies' bonanza

If you really want to find out whether it's true what they say about rabbits, just try a glass of Bunnies' Bonanza. The traditional aphrodisiac benefits of coriander and celery, the sexual stimulus of parsley and the plant oestrogens in cabbage make this the perfect potion for couples.

carrots 3, unpeeled; unless organic, remove top and bottom
cabbage 2 dark-green leaves
celery 1 stick, with leaves
coriander 1 handful
parsley 1 handful, with stems

vital statistics
Super-rich in vitamins A and C. *Rich* in sulphur. *Contains* some calcium and iron. It's the phytochemicals that work in this mixture. The potent volatile oils in coriander and celery, and the strengthening indoles in cabbage are the key – which is probably why cabbage is known as the medicine of the poor throughout Europe. The antiviral benefit of carrots and the anti-bacterial properties of coriander also make sure there'll be no bugs in your bunny.

asparadisia

There are pictures of cultivated asparagus in 6,000-year-old Egyptian tombs, and it has been used medicinally ever since. Whether its reputation as an aphrodisiac comes merely from its shape or from its chemical constituents is unclear, but it has been accorded this attribute by civilizations throughout the world. Combined here with the fortifying strength of broccoli and watercress, this is the most health-giving of drinks.

asparagus 6 spears
carrots 2, unpeeled; unless organic, remove top and bottom
broccoli 1 head, florets only
watercress 1 handful

vital statistics

Super-rich in vitamins A, C, folic acid and potassium. *Contains* iron, calcium and phosphorous. Surprisingly, asparagus contains substantial amounts of protein for a vegetable – as much, in fact, as the same weight of rice, corn on the cob, or a bean and vegetable casserole. The slow-release energy from this protein and the combined constituents of the other vegetables make Asparadisia your gateway to paradise.

Even in the best-ordered lives there are times when hauling yourself out of bed requires a superhuman effort. There are days where energy seems so lacking that the thought of getting dressed and dragging yourself to work is enough to bring on an instant attack of doom and gloom. I call this

pick-me-up

TTFN (Total but Temporary Fatigue Neurosis), and 75 per cent of the population say they wake up with it at some time. Of course, the more common causes of TTFN are self-inflicted: too much booze the night before, burning the candle at both ends, an endless diet of junk food, sticky buns and sweets. Yet many people suffer TTFN through no fault of their own. They are simply ground down by the stresses and pressures of modern life, jobs and children; illness or infection; poor absorption of nutrients due to digestive problems; or other physical disorders such as Seasonal Affective Disorder (SAD), ME, or chronic fatigue syndrome. Even in the absence of all these problems, however, nutritional deficiencies are frequently the cause of TTFN.

Intensively grown crops raised on poor soil, intensively farmed animals reared in far from ideal circumstances, even apparently good food so processed that it loses substantial amounts of its original value... all of these things eventually take their toll.

juices

One universally ignored cause of TTFN is the depletion of nutrients and other vital substances that results from long-term use of prescribed and over-the-counter medicines. Many doctors are unaware of the damaging effects some medicines have on nutritional well-being (*see* 'Chemical Robbery', page 142).

These are just some of the reasons that so many people need a pick-me-up, and there's no better way to get one than with a glass of freshly made juice. For extra potency, some of the juices in this section are fortified by the addition of such power-packing nutrients as wheat germ, molasses, nuts and seeds, dried fruits, maple syrup, honey, soya milk, tofu, kelp and vitamins.

c-plus

C-Plus is just the thing to boost your natural resistance and give you that extra 'get up and go' if you're feeling a bit more than one degree under par. Echinacea is a plant that is native to North America but now grows widely throughout Europe. It has been used for centuries by herbalists for its specific ability to support and enhance the body's own immune system. To create this Pick-me-up Juice, use a one-gram soluble vitamin C tablet, dissolve it in a little water, add the echinacea extract, stir into the finished juice and drink immediately. You can find both the vitamin C tablets and echinacea at chemists or good health-food stores.

oranges 2, peeled, leaving pith behind
*grapefruit 1, peeled, leaving pith behind
key lime 1, unpeeled
vitamin c 1 one-gram tablet
echinacea extract 30 drops

If taking prescribed medicines, consult your doctor before drinking large amounts of grapefruit juice

vital statistics

Doubly *Super-rich* in vitamin C: a glass of C-Plus is equivalent to a whole week's requirement. The abundant bioflavonoids from the citrus fruits make this juice a superb free-radical scavenger which cleans up the system as well as providing excellent Superjuice protection.

super stinger

Make sure you wear gloves when gathering the stinging nettles, but don't worry – the juice won't sting. Nettles have been used as medicine since the earliest times and were one of the favourite herbs of the first-century Greek physician Dioscorides. This powerful herb, combined with the immune-boosting benefits of carrots and spinach, makes this an instant tonic.

carrots 3, unpeeled; unless organic, remove top and bottom
apples 2, unpeeled, uncored and quartered
stinging nettles 1 bunch young, pale-green
spinach 1 handful of leaves

vital statistics

Super-rich in vitamin A. *Rich* in vitamin C. *Contains* calcium, potassium and iron. The flavonoids in spinach and nettles boost Super Stinger's protective value, while the vitamin C from the apples improves absorption of its iron content. This is an ideal juice for nursing mothers as it increases the flow of breast milk, guards against anaemia and restores energy.

vital statistics

Super-rich in vitamin C and potassium. *Contains* useful amounts of calcium. It's not just the vitamin C content that is so important in this recipe, it's the wide range of protective flavonoids which helps increase natural immunity against both bacteria and viruses, and plays a major part in protecting the body against cancer. As a bonus, you'll also get a substantial shot of folic acid and some useful vitamin A.

grapefruit glitz

When peeling the grapefruit and oranges to make this fruit-packed Superjuice, be sure to leave plenty of the white pith still attached to the flesh, as this is where this tonic's bioflavonoids are found. If you're lucky enough to find very thin-skinned lemons, there's no need to peel them at all – though it's best to taste a little of the peel first, as this can sometimes be very bitter.

*grapefruit 2, peeled, leaving pith behind
oranges 2, peeled, leaving pith behind
lemon 1, with peel if thin-skinned

*If taking prescribed medicines, consult your doctor before drinking large amounts of grapefruit juice

vital statistics

Super-rich in vitamin C and folic acid. *Contains* vitamin A, iron, calcium and masses of potassium. This Superjuice is also a good source of protective flavonoids. Lettuce contains substances known as lactones, and was used by the ancient Assyrians as a mild sedative. All of which makes the Life Saver an ideal calming and restorative juice for children recovering from illness.

life saver

Just the juice to revive that sinking feeling! Of all the lettuces, iceberg probably has the least amount of nutrients – especially when compared with the dark-green and red leafed varieties. However, it doesn't go slimy in your fridge after three days; in fact, it will keep well for two weeks if wrapped in cling film. It has a much sweeter flavour than other lettuce and contains the highest levels of natural calming substances. If you're tense, anxious and irritable, as well as being run down, then this is the cure.

apples 3, unpeeled, uncored and quartered
oranges 2, peeled, leaving pith behind
lemon 1, with peel if thin-skinned
iceberg lettuce 2 handfuls

entente cordiale

This combination of the typically British carrot and beetroot with the sunny Mediterranean flavour of basil combines the best of northern and southern European flavours. The blood-building benefits of beetroot contrast delightfully with the cooling flavour of cucumber, while the energy-giving natural sugars in the root vegetables blend wonderfully with the heady aroma, digestive benefits and mentally stimulating effects of basil.

carrots 3, unpeeled; unless organic, remove top and bottom
beetroot 1 medium, unpeeled, with leaves
cucumber ½ medium
basil 1 handful of leaves

vital statistics

Super-rich in vitamin A.
Rich in folic acid and potassium.
Contains vitamin C, magnesium and calcium. It isn't just the obvious protective nutrients that make this juice a pick-me-up, but the content of betaine (an anthocyanin) in beetroot which improves the quality of the blood. Like so many herbs, basil has an ancient history as a medicine and, whether taken in this juice or used in cooking, it energises both mind and body.

welsh ginger

Is it coincidence that the national emblem of Wales is a leek? The Welsh are renowned for their wonderful male-voice choirs – and leeks have been used to soothe, protect and improve the quality of the voice since Roman times. Even so, it's not for its vocal properties that the leek is combined here with carrots, parsley and ginger. Like its close relatives, garlic and onions, the leek boosts immunity and stimulates energy. Combined with the ginger, it makes this a guaranteed pep-up recipe.

carrots 4, unpeeled; unless organic, remove top and bottom
leek 1 small
parsley 1 handful, with stems
ginger ½ oz fresh root

vital statistics

Super-rich in vitamin A, beta-carotene and other vital carotenoids. *Rich* in potassium. *Contains* vitamin C and calcium. The phytochemicals in the leek stimulate good digestion and improve nutrient absorption to increase energy levels. The gentle diuretic effects of parsley help eliminate toxins (especially after illness), while the ginger stimulates circulation and perks up the entire system.

stir-fry starter

Here is everything you get in an oriental restaurant, without the wok. Like our home-grown savoy cabbage, these exotic relatives – Chinese cabbage and Pak Choi – are members of the *cruciferae* family. Their flavours blend perfectly with those of carrots and sweet potato. The rich mineral content of seaweed is a vital addition to this recipe, while sesame seeds supply both energy and that elusive oriental flavour. Anyone suffering or recovering from serious illness will benefit from this powerful pick-me-up. Sprinkle the sesame seeds onto the finished juice for a massive energy, vitamin and mineral bonus.

carrots 2, unpeeled; unless organic, remove top and bottom
sweet potato 1 small, unpeeled
chinese cabbage ½ medium
pak choi 1 handful
seaweed 1 handful (wash to remove salt)
sesame seeds 2 teaspoons

vital statistics

Super-rich in vitamins A, C, E, carotenoids, folic acid and potassium. *Contains* some B vitamins, iron, magnesium and iodine. This juice is bursting with the phytochemicals which encourage detoxification, work powerfully against hormone-related cancers and protect against cell damage in general. Hence, Stir-fry Starter is ideal for anyone suffering from ME, chronic fatigue, overwork or just plain tiredness.

peppery pick-up

The instant energy from the molasses and the natural sugars in the apricots works hand-in-hand with the beneficial constituents of the other ingredients in this Pick-me-up Juice. The liver-activating properties of fennel stimulate the detoxifying process, while the cleansing effects of the peppers will soon get you back on your feet. This one also makes a great pick-me-up if you've had a drop too much of the hard stuff. Blend the finished juice with the molasses and apricots and a handful of ice-cubes for a delicious and stimulating cooler.

dried apricots 4, soaked overnight
oranges 2, peeled, leaving pith behind
fennel 1 medium bulb
red pepper ½, deseeded
yellow pepper ½, deseeded
molasses 1 dessertspoon

vital statistics
Super-rich in vitamins A and C, carotenoids, potassium. *Contains* calcium, magnesium, phosphorus and iron.
Peppery Pick-up is especially healing to the stomach thanks to the fennel, a vegetable long-used medicinally in southern Europe. The massive carotenoid content in this juice is a sure-fire recipe for rapid recovery. Its calcium, magnesium and potassium content also make it a great tonic after strenuous physical exercise.

on your mark

If you're putting off exercise because you just can't work up enough enthusiasm, this is the juice for you. On Your Mark is perfect before a round of golf, a game of tennis, an evening of ten-pin bowling, a session in the gym, a cycle ride or even just a long, brisk walk. The slow-release energy from the parsnip and carrots, the instant fruit sugars in the tangerines, and the sustaining benefits of the apple will certainly get you on your mark and raring to go.

tangerines 4, peeled
carrots 2, unpeeled; unless organic, remove top and bottom
apple 1, unpeeled, uncored and quartered
parsnip 1 large, unpeeled

vital statistics

Super-rich in vitamin C and beta-carotene. *Rich* in potassium, phosphorus, sulphur and silicon. *Contains* vitamin E and some B vitamins. The complex starches in the parsnip and carrots break down slowly, providing a gradual release of energy that is ideal for sporting activities. This juice will give you an instant lift and get you in the right frame of mind and body to enjoy any sporting interests.

ready, steady, go

If you've used 'On Your Mark' (page 84) and it's given you enough of a boost to start thinking about exercise, then this is the juice to really get you up and going. It combines masses of energy from the pears, kiwi fruit and wheat germ with the super-protection against free radicals derived from the watercress and the soya yoghurt. This is the ideal regular juice when you're feeling a bit down but really want to be more active. It's great for everyone but particularly good for women, as soya helps control hormone fluctuations.

pears 2, unpeeled
kiwi fruit 1, unpeeled
broccoli 4 oz, florets only
soya yoghurt 1 carton
wheat germ 2 tablespoons
watercress 1 bunch

vital statistics

Super-rich in vitamin C. *Rich* in beta-carotene and carotenoids. *Contains* iron, sulphur, vitamin E and protein. As well as the generally protective benefits of all the carotenoids and the vitamin C, this juice is rich in phytochemicals from the broccoli and the watercress which are extremely important for the protection of lung tissue against cancer. The vitamin E in wheat germ helps the circulation and will keep you ahead of the field no matter what your chosen sport.

wake-up whammy

Here's a Pick-me-up Juice with a vengeance. Make sure you choose the ripest possible tomatoes, as that's when they're at their most nutritious. Most people don't realise that tomatoes are a member of the *Solenaceae* family, which includes potatoes, peppers and aubergines; they're all relatives of the nightshade. For this reason, this juice is not ideal for anyone with rheumatoid arthritis, though it's not a problem if you have osteoarthritis. To make it, stir the kelp powder (you can find it in most good health-food shops) into the juice just before drinking.

tomatoes 4 medium
sweet potato 1 small, unpeeled
ginger 1 oz fresh root
celery 2 sticks, with leaves
kelp powder 2 teaspoons

vital statistics

Super-rich in vitamin C, beta-carotene, lycopene and iodine. *Contains* potassium and folic acid. As well as all the protective benefits of the carotenoids and vitamin C, this juice also contains some coumarin compounds from the celery which pep up the entire circulatory system, boost the protective function of white cells and lower blood pressure. The kelp powder is rich in iodine, which stimulates the thyroid and gets your body working in overdrive.

buzz juice

In this recipe, the tropical fruits alone would make a truly wonderful Pick-me-up Juice, but once you add guarana, you'll be buzzing. The Rain Forest Indians in Brazil discovered guarana, and I've learned what a wonderful energy-giver this strange berry can be. Guarana isn't a quick shot in the arm and a let-down half an hour later; it supplies is a slow release of energy over several hours (you can find it in most good health-food shops). To make Buzz Juice, juice all fruits except the banana (look for mangosteens in supermarkets in season), then liquidize with the banana, guarana extract and a handful of ice cubes. Drink immediately.

mango 1, peeled, without stone
guava 1, peeled
passion-fruit 1, flesh scooped into juicer
mangosteen 1, cut in half, flesh scooped into juicer
banana 1, peeled
guarana 15 ml of extract

vital statistics
Super-rich in vitamin C, carotenoids and potassium. *Contains* B vitamins and folic acid. All the tropical fruits supply antioxidants and are highly protective, but they also contain an abundance of natural enzymes. These substances speed up the healing process after surgery or injury; they also stimulate the immune system, and some are involved in the conversion of carbohydrates into usable energy for the body. It's impossible to feel low for long once you start to get the buzz from this unique and beautifully flavoured drink.

The human body should survive in an active, healthy state for 120 years, but as most of us know, it rarely does. However, in parts of the world where longevity is taken for granted – by the Hunza tribesmen in the Himalayas, the Lamas of Tibet, the Fakirs of India – diets are rich in nuts,

protective

berries, fruits and fermented milk products. Today we all have access to the concentrated protective power of these natural foods in the form of Protective Juices.

Many years ago, I spent a few days working with one of the most famous nutritional healers of modern times, Gaylord Hauser, who numbered most of the great Hollywood stars of the Forties, Fifties and Sixties among his clients. He was convinced that a daily pint of fresh juice was the best safeguard against illness and premature ageing.

Certainly, the vegetables and fruits that go into such juices contain a protective anti-cancer cocktail we cannot afford to ignore. Tragically, however, during a typical week, three-quarters of adults don't eat a single piece of citrus fruit, half of them don't eat an apple or a pear, and two-thirds don't touch any type of green vegetable. For maximum protection against cancer as well as general health benefits, we should all eat a wide variety of fresh produce and drink at least one glass of fresh juice daily.

juices

Everyone knows that fruits, salads and vegetables contain vitamins and minerals, but few are aware of their powerful protective constituents. Natural plant substances known as phytochemicals play a major part in the protective action of these foods against cancers and other diseases, and they do so in a variety of ways. Carrots and green vegetables, for example, protect against lung cancer, while it has been shown that increased consumption of fruit lowers the risk of mouth and throat cancers.

The Protective Juices in this chapter allow you to create your own glassful of these and other vital cancer-fighters. Incorporated as a regular part of your health regime, the following recipes could literally protect your life.

long-life lemonade

Sauerkraut might sound like a strange thing to juice, but this pickled cabbage is used as a traditional East European protective medicine against stomach ulcers and cancer. Combined with the cancer-fighting properties of beetroot and carrots, as well the apple's natural pectin fibre (which protects the heart and circulation), it makes this juice very special. It tastes much better than it sounds, too, since the sauerkraut's slightly acidic flavour is offset by the sweetness of the other ingredients.

carrots 3, unpeeled; unless organic, remove top and bottom
radishes 3, medium, with leaves if possible
apples 2, unpeeled, uncored and quartered
lemon 1, with peel if thin-skinned
beetroot 1 medium, with leaves
sauerkraut 2 tablespoons

vital statistics
Super-rich in beta-carotene, vitamin C, potassium and folic acid. *Contains* calcium and iron. The massive potassium content of beetroot with its leaves helps keep blood pressure low – vital for a long and active life. The radishes are specifically healing to the mucous membranes of the nose, sinuses and throat while protecting against chest infections.

cucumber soother

This Protective Juice helps to prevent as well as cure sore throats, tonsillitis, laryngitis and sinusitis. How? Well, the healing properties of carrots combine well with the soothing effect of cucumber on the mucous membranes, and the diuretic action of celery reduces swelling of the tonsils, adenoids and throat. Add sage, which is powerfully antiseptic and a traditional remedy for all mouth and throat problems, and you have some real ammunition against the woes of winter.

carrots 3, unpeeled; unless organic, remove top and bottom
celery 2 sticks, with leaves
pineapple 1 small
sage 6 fresh leaves
cucumber 6 inches

vital statistics

Super-rich in beta-carotene, potassium and natural enzymes. *Contains* vitamin C and folic acid. The natural enzyme bromelain in pineapple is especially healing to the lining of the mouth and throat; it is also a great aid to digestion, so it maximises the extraction of nutrients from foods. Sage is a valuable antiseptic due to its high content of the essential oil known as thujone.

Rich in potassium and vitamin C. The real value of this Protective Juice lies in the phytochemicals it contains. Ellagic acid from the apples has powerful anti-cancer qualities, while coumarins in the celery also protect against cancer, reduce blood pressure and act as a tonic to the circulatory system. Combined with the antifungal, anti-bacterial and heart-protective substances in garlic, they make for an excellent glassful of protection.

dracula's delight

Just the juice to protect your blood and your immune system. Though Dracula is supposed to dislike garlic, it is certainly one of the most powerful of blood purifiers. At times of stress – physical or mental – the immune system is likely to suffer, leaving you prey to all sorts of marauding bugs. Dracula's Delight is the tonic you need at these times, but it's also good as a regular dose of health insurance, especially during the winter months.

apples 4, unpeeled, uncored and quartered
celery 2 sticks, with leaves
garlic 2 cloves, peeled

Super-rich in vitamins A, C and carotenoids. *Contains* folic acid, potassium and some calcium. The very high vitamin A content in carrots and tomatoes, together with the wide selection of other carotenoids and lycopenes, offer specific protection against cancers of the mouth and throat. The sulphur content in radishes is anti-bacterial and their bitter flavour stimulates the flow of saliva – crucial to the prevention of gum disease.

good mouthkeeping

More people lose their teeth through gum disease than tooth decay. Naturally, there's no substitute for proper mouth care and regular visits to your dentist and hygienist. However, smoking, alcohol and very hot drinks can all damage the delicate tissues inside the mouth and throat – which is why this juice is designed specifically to protect those sensitive areas.

radishes 6, with leaves
carrots 4, unpeeled; unless organic, remove top and bottom
tomatoes 4 medium
spring onion 1 medium
leek 6 inches, cut lengthways in strips
Optional: Worcestershire sauce and fresh-ground black pepper to taste

pro-bonus 1

The earlier women start to build healthy bones, the less likely they are to develop osteoporosis in later life. The Superjuices Pro-bonus 1 and 2 are good sources of easily absorbed calcium and magnesium, both of which are essential for bone development. They're a great bone tonic for women throughout life – but don't forget that some men also develop osteoporosis, so it's good for them, too.

apples 3, unpeeled, uncored and quartered
celery 2 sticks, with leaves
beetroot 1 medium, with leaves
cabbage ½ small round, cut in wedges

vital statistics
Super-rich in calcium, magnesium and vitamin C. *Rich* in folic acid and potassium. *Contains* iron and phosphorus. The extra nutrients from the beet tops, the cancer-fighting bonus of the nutrients in cabbage and the calming influences of celery make this Protective Juice a powerful tonic as well as a bone builder.

pro-bonus 2

This juice is not so rich in calcium as Pro-Bonus 1, but it does provide a treasure trove of other micronutrients that are vital for the formation of healthy bones. Pro-Bonus 2 is ideal at any age, but it is especially good for women approaching, going through or after the menopause, as it ensures the best utilisation of other calcium sources in the diet.

carrots 4, unpeeled; unless organic, remove top and bottom
chard leaves 3 large , with stalks
apples 2, unpeeled, uncored and quartered
broccoli 2 small heads purple sprouting, with leaves and stems
red pepper 1 small, deseeded and quartered
watercress 1 handful, with stalks

vital statistics

Super-rich in vitamins A, C, E, B$_6$, folic acid, potassium and magnesium. *Contains* vitamin K, calcium, boron, some other B vitamins and iron. Just consuming large quantities of calcium on its own is not the answer to life-long strong and healthy bones. It's vital to include the trace minerals and vitamins that are essential to this complex process – and this Superjuice has an abundance of them all.

soy salsa

If this drink were a drug, it would be hailed as 'a breakthrough' by the modern pharmaceutical industry! Its heart and artery-protecting traits combine the kick of a Mexican mule with the cancer-fighting properties of the soya bean; for those with a more delicate digestion, there are also the stomach-soothing benefits of mint. As if that weren't enough, Soy Salsa also guards against joint damage and chest infections.

mint 6 leaves
spring onions 2 medium
tomatoes 2 medium
jalapeño pepper 1 small, deseeded
garlic 1, peeled
cucumber ½ medium
soya milk 4 oz, stir into finished juice

vital statistics
Rich in vitamin A. *Contains* vitamin C, potassium, folic acid. Here's another Superjuice that is more valuable for its phytochemicals than for its vitamin and mineral content. Jalapeño peppers, tomatoes, garlic, onions, mint and soya milk contain (respectively) substances which protect against joint disease, heart disease, bacterial and fungal infections, high blood pressure, digestive upsets and breast cancer. What more could you ask?

skin deep

Helena Rubenstein once said, 'Never put anything on your face that you wouldn't put in your mouth.' Well, this juice is far too good to waste on the outside, as it's not only a skin healer and cleanser but a powerful skin protector. Beauty is definitely more than skin deep, and it's pointless wasting time and money on lotions and potions if you're not feeding the skin with everything it needs from within.

carrots 4, unpeeled; unless organic, remove top and bottom
asparagus 2 spears
iceberg lettuce ½ medium
spinach 1 handful of leaves

vital statistics

Super-rich in vitamins A, C, beta-carotene and folic acid. *Rich* in iron and vitamin E. *Contains* potassium, silica and some B vitamins. Not only does it protect against skin infections thanks to its high vitamin A and beta-carotene content, Skin Deep also provides plenty of vitamin E, which helps maintain supple and wrinkle-free skin. This juice is also a blood builder – which means more skin nutrients are carried to the surface where they're needed.

vital statistics

Super-rich in vitamin A, beta-carotene and other essential carotenoids. *Contains* vitamins C and E, folic acid and iron.

The old wives' tale that carrots help you see in the dark is true. Beta-carotene is essential for proper night vision, and other carotenoids, such as lutein and xeaxanthine in spinach and kale, also protect against AMD (*see* below). This is a juice to drink regularly for long-term eye health and protection.

eye brite

In these days of computers, VDUs, and TV-watching, it has never been more important to protect the eyes. The most common cause of poor sight and blindness in elderly people is Age-related Macular Degeneration, or AMD. The latest evidence shows that this disease tends to coincide with a low intake of specific carotenoids. People who consistently eat foods containing these protective substances are at much lower risk of getting AMD.

carrots 4, unpeeled; unless organic, remove top and bottom
kale 2 leaves
watercress 1 bunch
parsley 1 small handful , with stems
spinach 1 handful of leaves

vital statistics

Super-rich in vitamin C, bioflavonoids, potassium, beneficial live bacteria and healthy calories. The dark-coloured pigments in blackcurrants give a healthy boost to the body's own natural defences as well as protection against some cancers. The live beneficial bacteria from the yoghurt not only ensure good digestion, but are also known to play a vital part in the immune process.

back to school

Put the fruit juice in a blender with the banana, yoghurt, honey and echinacea to make this great immune booster. It's terrific at any time, but give your children an extra three glasses of this juice in the week before they go back to school. They're going to come into contact with all sorts of bugs they haven't encountered during the holidays or before starting school. This Superjuice offers protection against bacteria and viruses, and will help keep them illness-free. By the way: it works for parents, too!

tangerines 3, peeled (or satsumas or clementines)
pineapples ½, sliced, with skin
blackcurrants 4 oz (fresh or frozen)
banana 1, peeled
yoghurt 1 carton, live
runny honey 1 dessertspoon
echinacea 10 drops herbal extract

vital statistics

Super-rich in vitamins A, C, folic acid *and* potassium. *Contains* iron, magnesium, calcium, *some* vitamin E *and* B vitamins. Nothing could be better than Savoir Vivre as a regular once-a-week boost to the immune system. Its high vitamin C content makes the minerals much more easily absorbed, and the volatile oils in ginger and garlic are key factors in protecting against heart and circulatory disease.

savoir vivre

You'll get super-power protection from this recipe. The combined properties of garlic and ginger for heart and circulation, the infection-fighting benefits of the artichoke, and the general immune benefits of melon and chicory make this Superjuice one of the best all-round protectors there is.

carrots 3, unpeeled; unless organic, remove top and bottom
jerusalem artichokes 2, scrubbed but unpeeled
garlic 1 clove, peeled
chicory 1 small head
melon ½ small yellow, deseeded, sliced, with peel
ginger ½ oz fresh root

Super-rich in vitamins A, C, E, carotenoids, potassium.
Rich in B$_6$, folic acid, magnesium, iron, and other B vitamins. This is a meal in a glass, but it's not just the conventional nutrients which make Doctor Garlic so valuable. The enormous protective benefits of garlic cover heart, circulation, chest infections, other bacteria and fungi. Ginger also protects the heart and, together with the jalapeño pepper, the joints, too. Mooli, the white radish, is one of the great liver protectors.

doctor garlic

This Superjuice may not win friends and influence people, and it is not for the faint-hearted, but Doctor Garlic represents the ultimate in veggie power. It is a Superjuice which exploits the pick of the protective vegetables with the kick of garlic, mooli and jalapeño. An all-year-round immune booster with massive built-in protection, it tastes seriously better than it sounds –but make sure you drink it with the one you love.

garlic 3 cloves, peeled
carrots 2, unpeeled; unless organic, remove top and bottom
celery 1 stick, with leaves
tomato 1 medium
sweet potato 1, scrubbed, unpeeled, cut into sticks
jalapeño pepper ½, deseeded
mooli (white radish) 3 inches

Since ancient times, man has made and enjoyed alcoholic drinks, from the most primitive fermented beer to wine and distilled spirits. Alcohol has played a major part in religious ceremonies, has been used medicinally and for celebration, but nothing else has polarised populations as

booze

the arguments for and against the plain enjoyment of booze. In Victorian times, anti-alcohol campaigners battled against 'demon drink' – so much so, in fact, that Victorian women perpetuated the myth that eating cheese late at night caused nightmares in order to stop their menfolk drinking the port that went with the Stilton. In the US, Prohibition proved to be a disaster as well as a failure – and it certainly didn't stop anybody from drinking if they wanted to do so. So what is the truth about alcohol? The best dietary advice in decades is the idea that a couple of glasses of wine a day protect us all against heart disease. Statistics show that the life expectancy of total abstainers is somewhat less than that of moderate social drinkers.

No one can argue against the very real dangers of excessive alcohol consumption, but sticking to the guidelines of 14 units of alcohol a week for women and 21 for men appears to pose no risk and seems to convey considerable benefits. One 'official' unit of

juices

alcohol is the equivalent of a small glass of wine, a pub measure of spirits or half a pint of normal-strength beer. Contrary to what most people believe, however, alcohol is a depressant – not a stimulant. Yet it is the way in which alcohol depresses the inhibitory centres of the brain that gives it its relaxing and mood-enhancing properties. That is why these Booze Juices have been included in this book: they are a collection of delicious recipes designed for special, relaxing moments. They also supply a shot of antioxidants to protect you against the damaging effects of alcohol, and give you a glassful of healthy vitamins, minerals and other phytonutrients into the bargain. Can you think of a better way to say 'Cheers'?

a hair of the dog

If you made the great mistake of having a night on the tiles, then this is probably what you need for that infamous morning after. Radishes help cleanse the liver. Carrots provide a massive boost of vitamin A (also good for the liver), and apples are among Nature's great detoxifiers.

carrots 6, unpeeled; unless organic, remove top and bottom
radishes 4, with leaves, if possible
apples 2, unpeeled, uncored and quartered
vodka 1 shot, stirred into finished juice

vital statistics

Super-rich in vitamin A, beta-carotene and other carotenoids. *Rich* in potassium. *Contains* vitamin C. This Superjuice is not only cleansing and healing to the liver, but the natural soluble fibre pectin from apples stimulates the digestive system and helps remove the alcoholic by-products from your body. Vodka, by the way, is one of the purest spirits available, and contains virtually no additives.

virgin fantasy

Here is an 'anytime cocktail' that combines the wonderful flavours of its ingredients with a modest alcoholic buzz. Add some black pepper and Worcestershire sauce if you like, and enjoy, knowing that you're doing your heart and kidneys a favour at the same time.

tomatoes 6 medium
carrots 2, unpeeled; unless organic, remove top and bottom
celery 1 stick, with leaves
parsley 1 handful, with stems
vodka 2 shots, stirred into finished juice

vital statistics

Super-rich in vitamin A and C, carotenoids and lycopene.
Rich in folic acid and potassium.
Its vitamin A content makes this a good Booze Juice for skin and eyes, as well as giving a boost to the immune system. The high content of lycopene also makes this a heart protector, and the combined effects of celery and parsley stimulate the activity of the kidneys.

vital statistics

Rich in vitamin C. Not a terrific
source of any other nutrients, but
the Healer Colada does contain an
abundance of a remarkable enzyme called
bromelane. This constituent speeds
up digestion – especially of all types of
meat – and it also has the ability to break
down any blood clots that might be
forming in the circulatory system.
Add the modest dose of alcohol, and
you're really taking care of your heart.

healer colada

If you need an excuse for this delicious drink, then tell your friends it's great
for sore throats (as well as being a tasty cure for indigestion). Surprisingly, the
Healer Colada also guards against the formation of blood clots, so it is
protective against both strokes and heart disease. To make it, first juice
the pineapple, then stir in the coconut milk and rum.

pineapple 1 medium, unpeeled but remove top
coconut milk 6 oz
white rum 2 oz

pink punch

This pink delight has universal taste appeal. The subtle blends of sweet flavours from the strawberries and cherries mingle with the tartness of the cranberries and grapefruit to produce an exceptionally clean-tasting, refreshing juice. Though alcohol isn't ideal for anyone with cystitis, if you must booze, then this is the juice to choose.

*pink grapefruit 1, peeled, but leaving the pith behind
cherries 6 oz, stoned
cranberries 6 oz
strawberries 6 oz
vodka 2 shots, stirred into finished juice

*If taking prescribed medicines, consult your doctor before drinking large amounts of grapefruit juice

quick, quick, sloe

If anything is guaranteed to get your feet tapping, it is this Booze Juice.
Instant energy, instant sunshine in a glass, instant pleasure... all this and
more from this exotic combination of nutrient-rich fruits and the unusual
flavour of sloe gin. If you can't make your own sloe gin, don't worry;
you'll find it in the shops. This juice is beneficial for the skin, eyes
and digestion – and for good measure, it's an immune booster, too.

apricots 6, stoned
oranges 2, peeled, but leaving the pith behind
peaches 2, stoned
mango 1, peeled and stoned
sloe gin 2 shots, stirred into finished juice

vital statistics

Super-rich in **vitamins A** and C.
Contains **potassium, calcium,
magnesium**. Although Quick, Quick,
Sloe contains valuable vitamins, it's really
the enzymes and protective chemicals
that make it such a good juice. Besides
its other benefits, it's helpful for fighting
chest infections and is also a good juice
for anyone with high blood pressure.
As if that weren't enough, sloe gin – a
traditional homemade country liquor
using wild fruit from the blackthorn bush
– is also a remedy for diarrhoea.

whisky mcvital

Whether you're going down with a cold or flu, or getting over either, this is the perfect comfort drink. When the Scots invented whisky, they named it *uisge beatha*, Gaelic for 'water of life' – and they weren't wrong. Combined with the ginger, especially as a hot toddy, the warming benefits of Whisky McVital are instantly apparent. But it does you good, too, thanks to the nutritional value of the fruit juices.

oranges 2, peeled, leaving the pith behind
lime 1, peeled, unless key lime
lemon 1, peeled
white grapes 6 oz
ginger ½ oz fresh root
whisky 2 shots, stirred into finished juice
boiling water optional; add to make a hot toddy

vital statistics

Super-rich in vitamin C and bioflavonoids. *Contains* carotenoids and calcium. As well as the immune-boosting, defensive properties of this very high dose of vitamin C, Whisky McVital also contains gingerols from the ginger, which stimulate the circulation and produce a strong expectorant effect which helps if you've got a cough.

kentucky comforter

This southern comforter conjures up images of American colonial verandas, rocking chairs and hot, lazy evenings. It's just the thing as an after-dinner drink to improve the digestion, settle the stomach and ensure a good night's sleep, free from heartburn. Fresh mint is best of all natural antacids, and its flavour combines perfectly with the bourbon. Drink deep, y'all!

apples 6, unpeeled, uncored and quartered

mint 6 fresh leaves

sweet potato 1 medium, cut in strips

bourbon 2 shots, stirred into juice and poured over plenty of ice-cubes

vital statistics

Super-rich in vitamins A and C. *Contains* other carotenoids, potassium, phosphorus. Pectin from the apples – a natural form of soluble fibre – aids the digestion. Together with the ellagic acid (also from apples), it improves the body's powers of elimination. Sweet potato adds lots of healthy beta-carotene (along with the traditional flavours of the South). The aromatic oils in mint are the perfect protector against digestive discomfort. They increase the flow of bile to improve fat digestion, and relax the muscles of the stomach and colon.

rain forest freezer

I was floating through the Brazilian rain forest in a small boat on the Amazon when I had my first taste of Caipirinha – the national cocktail of Brazil. It's traditionally made from a white rum distilled from sugar cane called *cachaça*, chopped limes and lots of ice and sugar. In the overwhelming heat and humidity of the rain forest, its cool and refreshing and tastes like lemonade. Beware! Its effects creep up on the uninitiated.

lime 1, unpeeled
papaya 1, peeled and deseeded
pineapple 1, thick slice, unpeeled
Juice the above
cachaça 2 shots (or other white rum)
guarana 2 teaspoons of extract
lime 1, unpeeled, cut in small pieces
sugar 2 teaspoons sugar
Put plenty of ice in a large glass.
Add the above ingredients,
then pour in the juice and stir.

vital statistics
Super-rich in vitamin C. *Rich* in vitamin A and carotenoids. Bring a little sunshine into a dull, rainy day with this wonderful cocktail. Naturally, it's also a great drink on a hot summer's afternoon and the slow-release energy from the guarana will help offset the almost irresistible desire to have 'just one more'. The Brazilian rain forest Indians have used the amazing properties of the guarana seed for more than a thousand years to help them survive the rigours of jungle life.

Super-rich in vitamins A, C, E, folic acid and potassium. *Contains* calcium, magnesium, niacin and vitamin B$_6$. This is a good anti-cancer cocktail, thanks to the cabbage and beetroot. It also provides a gentle diuretic effect, thanks to the celery, and the high content of vitamins A and E means that it's good for the circulation and skin, too. The volatile oils from caraway seeds are known to act directly on the whole digestive system.

kummel kalma

Kummel is a clear, white spirit distilled from grain and flavoured with caraway seeds. It's widely popular in northern Europe as a digestif – especially in Holland where it originates. Combined here with the cleansing properties of this vegetable mixture, you have the ideal remedy for bloating, distension, wind and indigestion.

carrots 4, unpeeled; unless organic, remove top and bottom
cabbage 2 leaves
celery 2 sticks, with leaves if possible
apple 1, unpeeled, uncored and quartered
beetroot ½, unpeeled, with leaves
kummel 2 shots, stirred into finished juice

vital statistics

Super-rich in vitamin C and bioflavonoids. *Contains* B-complex vitamins, folic acid, manganese and iron. This Booze Juice is seriously curative. At the first signs of colds or flu take a large, hot glassful and an early night. The gingerols – volatile oils in ginger – open up the blood vessels and get your circulation whizzing round the body, increasing temperature and sweating. You'll feel great by the morning.

calvados cure-all

A universal cure-all for colds, flu, headache, backache, toothache, rheumatism, lethargy, listlessness, or for anyone who is just plain sick and tired of being sick and tired. The Calvados Cure-all is perfect after a day in the cold (or even a day when you can't be bothered to go out in the cold). The tonic effects of ginger and cloves and all the health benefits of apples and lemons complement the fiery zest of calvados, the traditional apple brandy of Normandy.

apples 2, unpeeled, uncored and quartered
lemons 2, with peel unless thin-skinned
cloves 2 whole
ginger 1 oz fresh root
honey 1 dessertspoon
calvados 2 shots, stirred into finished juice
boiling water enough to make a hot toddy

Shakes and Smoothies may sound like little more than a tasty indulgence, but nothing could be further from the truth. They can be a meal in a glass, a convalescent's first steps on the road to recovery, a vegetable-hating child's salvation and the busy person's brilliant alternative to instant TV dinners.

shakes and

The most unlikely but nutritionally excellent things can go into your blender – a far cry from the burger bar's high-fat, low-nutrient milkshakes. Some of these recipes need a blender (if you don't have one, then the hand-held magic wand types work fairly well, even if they take a bit longer). Others require a juicer and a blender. Don't be put off by the need for equipment: believe me, these Superjuices are honestly worth the effort and the washing up.

Milk, yoghurt and frozen yoghurt, soya milk and yoghurt, ice-cream of all types (including soya), fruits, dried fruits, nuts, seeds, fortifying nutritional ingredients such as wheat germ, lecithin, brewer's yeast, kelp, molasses, even vitamin C... all are included in the following Shake and Smoothie recipes. However, the ingredients can be tailored to your individual needs as well as tastes. Shakes and Smoothies also provide the ideal opportunity to include herbs and spices – especially those that have good effects on the digestive system. Nutmeg, cinnamon, cloves, ginger, mint and chillies are just a few examples.

smoothies

You'll find even more in the recipes themselves. Whether you need to gain or lose weight, Shakes and Smoothies can help, as each glassful provides a super-abundance of nutrients. What's more, this chapter includes recipes suitable for all ages – from toddlers to pensioners.

Of course, the idea of Shakes and Smoothies is nothing new. As devotees of Indian food know, drinks made from yoghurt are a favourite throughout India. They're ideal partners for hot, spicy food since capsaicin, the substance that makes chillies hot, dissolves in fat – not water. These recipes, however, are different from the typical Indian restaurant offerings, since the ingredients they contain are designed – as is everything in this book – specifically with good health in mind.

monkey business

This might sound like a kid's party treat – most children will love it – but it's also a real energy-boosting and nutritious Smoothie. Instantly available calories from the fruit sugar in the apples are mixed with the slower-release calories in the bananas to make this a suitable drink to take before sustained physical activity. As any athlete will tell you, bananas prevent cramp. Make sure you select one of the 'healthy' peanut butters, without added salt. To make it, juice the apples, then blend with the bananas and peanut butter.

apples 6, unpeeled, uncored and quartered
bananas 2, peeled
peanut butter 1 tablespoon smooth

vital statistics

Super-rich in vitamin C and potassium. *Contains* vitamin A. Apples provide large quantities of the soluble fibre pectin, which, together with the ulcer-fighting benefits of bananas, make this juice suitable for all digestive problems. The high content of ellagic acid from apples provides valuable cancer protection, and peanut butter supplies valuable protein, as well as iron, magnesium, vitamin E and folic acid.

jungle jive

A good start to any day is with the wide-awake flavours of mango and passion-fruit. Drink this for breakfast, followed by a bowl of wholegrain cereal or some wholemeal toast and honey, and you won't be craving sticky buns by the middle of the morning. To make it, first juice the mango and passion-fruit, then blend with the milk and yoghurt.

passion-fruit 2, flesh scooped out into juicer, with seeds
mango 1, peeled and stoned
frozen yoghurt 5 oz live, low-fat
skimmed milk 10 oz

vital statistics

Super-rich in calcium, potassium and flavonoids. *Contains* vitamins A and C. These tropical fruits are laden with protective antioxidants. Their high enzyme content is good for digestion; passion-fruit in particular is helpful in the relief of gout and arthritis. When combined with almost a day's requirement of calcium, mango and passion-fruit make this a fabulous morning mixture.

vital statistics

Super-rich in vitamin C, potassium, calcium, rich in B vitamins and vitamin E. *Contains* bioflavonoids, iron, magnesium. Abundant amounts of vitamin C are essential for healing and low intakes of this nutrient are known to delay wound-healing after surgery. If you've just had an operation, this shake will assist you on the road to a speedy recovery and protect you against infection into the bargain.

lime-e shake

A bonanza for blood and bones. Here's another shake with virtually a whole day's calcium needs, as well as the vitamin C you'd expect from citrus fruits. The bonus, however, comes from the wheat germ which simply oozes with B vitamins and vitamin E. Low in calories, high in antioxidants, Lime-E Shake should be the choice for anyone recovering from illness, or under excessive stress. To make it, first juice the oranges and lime, leaving as much pith on as possible, and then blend with the other ingredients.

oranges 2, peeled, leaving pith behind
lime 1, peeled (unless key lime)
banana 1, peeled
skimmed milk 10 oz
yoghurt 5 oz live, low-fat
wheat germ 2 heaped tablespoons

Super-rich in vitamins A, C and bioflavonoids. *Rich* in calcium. *Contains* some B vitamins, phosphorus, copper, iron and magnesium. The healing enzyme bromelain in the pineapple, the vitamin A in the mango and vitamin C with bioflavonoids in the lime make this one of the most comprehensive protectors around. Add the beneficial bacteria in yoghurt, and you'll see why Paradiso is one of the healthiest Smoothies you can drink.

paradiso

Just the aroma of mango, pineapple, lime and ginger is a transport to paradise. Drinking these juices is a passport to good health and vitality. Whipped into a cooling, frothy shake with live yoghurt, this combination is invigorating, restoring and protective. It's wonderful for children (though some prefer it without the ginger) and perfect in the early stages of pregnancy, as ginger helps prevent morning sickness. To make it, first juice the mango, pineapple, ginger and lime, then blend with the yoghurt and a handful of ice-cubes.

lime 1, peeled (unless key lime)
mango 1, peeled and stoned
pineapple 1, top removed
yoghurt 5 oz live, low-fat
ginger 1 oz fresh root

spiced silk

The historic use of both sesame and cumin goes back to ancient Egypt and China. Cumin is referred to in the Old Testament, and sesame seeds were found in the tomb of Tutankhamun. Both these seeds help improve the flow of breast milk in nursing mothers, and they are also digestive aids. When combined with the friendly bacteria in yoghurt, this is a powerfully effective shake. To make it, simply blend the yoghurt, tahini and cumin with a handful of ice-cubes, and sprinkle sesame seeds on top.

yoghurt 10 oz live, low-fat
tahini 1 tablespoon
sesame seeds 1 teaspoon
cumin seeds 1/2 teaspoon crushed

vital statistics
Rich in the B vitamin niacin, folic acid, calcium, zinc and vitamin E. *Contains* protein, and other B vitamins. Cumin seeds contain volatile oils, especially pinene and terpene, and it's these that have a direct action on the muscles of the gut. Sesame seeds are an excellent source of the health-giving linoleic acids, as well as containing lots of protein, calcium and other nutrients.

spice island special

You can almost imagine the sound of breakers on the coral reef when you smell the mixture of coconut, cinnamon and cloves. The addition of a shot of Jamaican rum is entirely optional, but totally delicious. This drink is of special value to women – though, of course, men can enjoy it, too. It's the amazing benefits of soya which protect against breast cancer that contribute to its value. To make it, blend all the ingredients with a handful of ice-cubes.

soya milk 10 oz
coconut milk 5 oz
frozen yoghurt 5 oz live, low-fat
ground cinnamon ½ teaspoon
ground cloves ¼ teaspoon

vital statistics

Contains protein, calcium, iron, some B vitamins. This shake is not included for normal nutritional reasons, although the small amounts of iron are better absorbed than that from most non-meat sources. The yoghurt provides a good source of calcium, while the cinnamon, cloves and beneficial bacteria are all digestive aids. It's really for the enormous cancer-fighting **benefits** present in all soya products that Spice Island Special should be drunk on a regular basis.

vital statistics

Super-rich in vitamins A, C, folic acid, potassium.
Contains some calcium, phosphorus and magnesium.

The Guardian is another powerful immune stimulator, not only due to its high content of vitamins A and C, but also to the coumarins in celery. These natural chemicals enhance the activity of white cells, an essential part of the body's natural defences. The heart-protecting lycopene from tomatoes combines with the all-round heart and circulatory protection gained from garlic.

the guardian

No vampire is going to sink their fangs into your neck after this garlic-laden tipple! But of course, garlic is powerfully antiseptic and wards off bugs as well as vampires. Mixed here with the heart-protective tomatoes and immune-boosting carrots, this Smoothie is the best excuse ever for a circulation-improving tipple. Enjoy it with a friend and a clear conscience. To make it, first juice the vegetables, then blend with crushed ice and vodka, and add the lemon chunks.

tomatoes 6 medium
carrots 2, unpeeled; unless organic, remove top and bottom
celery 2 sticks, with leaves
garlic 2 cloves, peeled
ice crushed
vodka 2 shots
lemon 1, with peel, cut in small chunks

Super-rich in vitamin C. *Rich* in potassium. *Contains* vitamin E. This Smoothie has a wide range of health benefits. It's good for digestion and constipation, and ideal for those suffering arthritis, rheumatism or gout. The lecithin helps improve brain function and memory, and the extra iron and potassium from molasses, together with the enormous amount of soluble fibre from the apples and pears, lowers cholesterol, reduces blood pressure and protects the heart.

agen provocateur

The best prunes in the world come from the small French town of Agen, where they've been grown for more than 800 years. *Pruneaux d'Agen* on the package means the same as *appellation contrôlée* on a bottle of fine wine. Prunes are famed for their gentle laxative action, but because of their high potassium content, they're good for high blood pressure, too. To make this Smoothie, first juice the apples and pears and purée the prunes in the blender, then add the juice, lecithin and molasses and blend together.

prunes	6, soaked and stoned
apples	4, unpeeled, uncored and quartered
pears	4, unpeeled
lecithin granules	1 dessertspoon
molasses	1 dessertspoon

green dream

If you're feeling a bit jaded, lacking in energy, and your skin's beginning to look tired, dry and wrinkly, serve up this Smoothie at least a couple of times a week. It lifts the spirits, thanks to the mood-enhancing effect of nutmeg, and the avocado works wonders on the skin without the surgeon's scalpel. To make Green Dream, put all the ingredients in the blender with a handful of ice-cubes.

avocado 1 large, peeled and stoned
kelp powder 1 dessertspoon
nutmeg generous grind
skimmed milk 10 oz
yoghurt 5 oz live, low-fat

Super-rich in calcium, vitamins E and B$_1$. *Rich* in folic acid and iodine. *Contains* protein and some vitamin D. Iodine is essential for the normal function of the thyroid gland, and few of the patients I see have a sufficient amount of this essential mineral in their diets. Deficiency can lead to chronic fatigue. It's not just the vitamin E in avocados that's good for the skin; they also contain natural chemicals that stimulate the production of collagen, which smoothes out the wrinkles and gives young skin its wonderful bloom.

mock mint choc

You don't have to wait till after eight to enjoy the delicious chocolate-mint flavour of this soya milkshake. You get all the nutritional benefits of carob without the fat and sugar content of chocolate. Masses of protein for long-term staying power, a quick energy boost from the honey and milk sugar in the yoghurt, together with the digestive benefits of mint make this an all-round winner. To create it, put the Brazil nuts in the blender first; when they're finely ground, add the other ingredients.

mint 6 leaves
brazil nuts 5, shelled
soya milk 10 oz
yoghurt 5 oz live, low-fat
honey 1 dessertspoon
carob powder 2 dessertspoons

vital statistics

Super-rich in calcium and selenium. *Rich* in protein and potassium. *Contains* iron.

As well as the amazing protection against breast cancer gained from soya milk, the Brazil nuts provide a whole day's needs of the trace mineral selenium. This much-ignored vital mineral is essential for normal functioning of the heart and for protection against prostate cancer. The average daily consumption in the UK is less than half the required amount.

body-builder

The world appears to be full of people trying to lose weight, but for the permanently skinny, life can be equally miserable. They won't go to the gym, the swimming pool or on beach holidays, and usually try stuffing themselves on unhealthy high-fat foods when what they really need is lots of small meals a day, including plenty of high-calorie, low-bulk foods like the ingredients in this super Shake. When I offered a weight-gain recipe in a national newspaper, we had 15,000 requests! To make the Body-builder, first purée the dates in the blender, then add all the other ingredients. Drink half in the morning, keep the rest in the 'fridge till evening.

dates 4 fresh, stoned
banana 1, peeled
molasses 1 dessertspoon
honey 1 dessertspoon
tahini 1 dessertspoon
wheat germ 1 dessertspoon
brewer's yeast 1 dessertspoon
whole milk 15 oz
yoghurt 5 oz live, full-fat

vital statistics

Super-rich in healthy calories, calcium and potassium. *Contains* iron, vitamin E and some B vitamins. Nuts, seeds, and dried fruits are a terrific source of calories with very little bulk. If you're underweight, it's extremely difficult to eat enough starchy foods to provide the surplus calories required. This Shake tastes great, and its added bonus comes from the dates, believed throughout the Middle East to have aphrodisiac properties. You've been warned!

skinny dip

If you need to lose weight, the one thing that doesn't work is going without food, feeling hungry and trying to stick to a very low-calorie diet. Reduce the amount of fat you consume and increase your physical activity: eat two slices of bread and butter a day less and walk 15 minutes a day more and you'll lose a pound a week. This Smoothie is filling, sustaining, nourishing, tasty and low in calories. To make it, simply juice the vegetables, then blend with other ingredients.

tomatoes 6 medium
celery 2 sticks, with leaves
parsley 1 handful, with stems
yoghurt 5 oz live, very low-fat
cottage cheese 4 oz very low-fat
brewer's yeast 2 teaspoons
worcestershire sauce to taste

vital statistics

Super-rich in vitamin C and carotenoids. *Rich* in calcium. *Contains* B vitamins, potassium and protein. Use Skinny Dip to replace one meal a day. The recipe will make a thick, creamy shake, but by adding more cottage cheese and less milk, you can make it thick enough to use as a dip. Eat it with a selection of crudités, such as celery, carrot, fennel, broccoli, cauliflower and peppers.

healing juices

As you'll have gathered by now, the fruits, vegetables, nuts, seeds and other ingredients used to make Superjuices are not included just because they taste good. Each and every one of them plays a fundamental role in helping to avoid and overcome a variety of illnesses. Even the most commonplace

the natural

ingredient is a pharmaceutical factory, manufacturing and storing hundreds of different substances known as *phyto-* ('plant') nutrients. These are not just the essential vitamins miraculously produced in leaves, roots, fruits, nuts and seeds; they also include complex chemical substances with specific health benefits.

For example: both vitamin A and the plant-based beta-carotene have specific cancer-fighting properties. Other carotenoids such as lutein, xeaxanthine and lycopene protect the eyes and heart. Vitamin C is best known for its antioxidant and protective powers, but studies around the world show that where diets are richest in foods containing vitamin C, people suffer less cancer. Until recently, vitamin E was thought essential only for animal reproductive function; there was no corresponding proof in humans. Today, we know that it is vital in the battle against heart disease. Similarly, deficiencies of folic acid, selenium and soluble fibre were once dismissed as relatively unimportant. It's now

pharmacy

known that these easily available nutrients can make the difference between good health or life-threatening disease. As well as the vitamin and mineral content of the nutrients listed in the following tables, you'll find frequent references to other phytochemicals in the *Superjuice* recipes. These are almost always complex substances now known to have undisputed cancer-fighting benefits. Nutrients in cruciferous vegetables; coloured pigments in berries, cherries and beetroot; limonene in citrus fruits... all these and many more exert unimaginable protective influences on human health. As I have said throughout this book, there is no better source of these phyto-nutrients than homemade, freshly prepared Superjuices. Making the most of them is up to you.

raw ingredients a-z

ingredient	source of:
Alfalfa sprouts	Calcium, silicon, vitamins A, B complex, C, E and K
Apples	Carotenes, ellagic acid, pectin, potassium, vitamin C
Apricots	Beta-carotene, iron, potassium, soluble fibre
Artichokes, Jerusalem	Inulin, iron, phosphorus
Asparagus	Asparagine, folic acid, potassium, phosphorus, riboflavin, vitamin C
Banana	Energy, fibre, folic acid, magnesium, potassium, vitamin A
Basil	Volatile oils: linalol, limonene, estragole
Beetroot	Beta-carotene, calcium, folic acid, iron, potassium, vitamins B_6 and C
Blackcurrants	anti-inflammatory and cancer-fighting phytochemicals, carotenoids, vitamin C
Blueberries	Anti-bacterial and cancer-fighting phytochemicals, carotenoids, vitamin C
Brazil nuts	Protein, selenium, vitamins B and E
Brewer's yeast	B vitamins, biotin, folic acid, iron, magnesium, zinc
Broccoli	Cancer-fighting phytochemicals, folic acid, iron, potassium, riboflavin, vitamins A and C
Cabbage family	Cancer-fighting phytochemicals, folic acid, potassium, vitamins A, C and E
Carrots	Carotenoids, folic acid, magnesium, potassium, vitamin A
Celery	Coumarins, potassium, vitamin C

ingredient	source of:
Chard (Swiss)	Calcium, cancer-fighting phytochemicals, carotenes, iron, phosphorus, vitamins A and C
Cherries	Cancer-fighting phytochemicals, flavonoids, magnesium, potassium, vitamin C
Chicory	Bitter, liver-stimulating terpenoids, folic acid, iron, potassium, vitamin A (if unblanched)
Chives	Beta-carotene, cancer-fighting phytochemicals, vitamin C
Cinnamon	Coumarins, tannins and volatile oils with mild, sedative/analgesic blood pressure-lowering effects
Cloves	Volatile oil (especially eugenol) with anti-nausea, antiseptic anti-bacterial and analgesic properties
Coconut milk	Calcium, magnesium, potassium, small quantities of B vitamins
Coriander	Coumarins, flavonoids, linalol
Cottage cheese	B vitamins, calcium, folic acid, magnesium, protein, vitamin A
Cranberries	Cancer-fighting phytochemicals, specific urinary anti-bacterials, vitamin C
Cucumber	Folic acid, potassium, silica, small amounts of beta-carotene in the skin
Cumin seeds	Flavonoids which relieve intestinal wind and spasm, volatile oils
Dandelion	Beta-carotene, diuretic and liver-stimulating phytochemicals, iron, other carotenoids
Dates	Fibre, folic acid, fruit sugar, iron, potassium
Fennel	volatile oils: fenchone, anethole and anisic acid, all liver and digestive stimulants
Figs	Beta-carotene, cancer-fighting phytochemicals, fibre, ficin (a digestive aid) iron, potassium

ingredient	source of:
Garlic	Anti-bacterial and antifungal sulphur compounds, cancer and heart disease-fighting phytochemicals
Ginger	Circulatory-stimulating zingiberene and gingerols
Grapes	Natural sugars, powerful antioxidant flavonoids, vitamin C
Grapefruit	Beta-carotene, bioflavonoids – especially naringin, which thins the blood and lowers cholesterol, vitamin C
Horseradish	Natural antibiotics, protective phytochemicals, vitamin C
Jalapeño pepper	Carotenoids, capsaicin: a circulatory stimulant, flavonoids
Kale	Beta-carotene, calcium, cancer-fighting phytochemicals, folic acid, iron, phosphorus, sulphur, vitamin C
Kiwi fruit	Beta-carotene, bioflavonoids, fibre, potassium, vitamin C
Kohlrabi	Cancer-fighting phytochemicals, folic acid, potassium, vitamin C
Lamb's lettuce	Folic acid, iron, potassium, vitamins A, C and B_6, zinc. Also contains calming phytochemicals
Lecithin	Phospholipids extracted from soya beans: heart protective and beneficial to nerves
Leeks	Anti-arthritic, anti-inflammatory substances, cancer-fighting phytochemicals, folic acid, potassium, diuretic substances, vitamins A and C
Lemon	Bioflavonoids, limonene, potassium, vitamin C
Lettuce	Calcium, folic acid, phosphorus, potassium, sleep-inducing phytochemicals, vitamins A and C
Lime	Bioflavonoids, limonene, potassium, vitamin C
Mango	Beta-carotene, flavonoids, potassium, other antioxidants, vitamin C

ingredient	source of:
Mangosteen	Digestive-friendly mucilage, potassium, vitamin C
Melon	Folic acid, potassium, small amounts of B vitamins, vitamins A and C
Milk	Calcium, protein, riboflavin, zinc
Mint	Antispasmodic volatile oils, flavonoids, menthol
Mixed salad leaves	Calcium, folic acid, phosphorus, potassium, sleep-inducing phytochemicals (the darkest leaves contain the most nutrients), vitamins A and C
Molasses	Calcium, iron, magnesium, phosphorus
Mooli	Iron, magnesium, phytochemicals that stimulate the gall bladder and heal mucous membranes, potassium, vitamin C
Nutmeg	Myristicin: mood enhancing and hallucinogenic in excess; phytochemicals that aid sleep and digestion
Oranges and citrus fruits (including mandarins, satsumas and tangerines)	Bioflavonoids, calcium, folic acid, iron, limonene, potassium, thiamine, vitamin B_6 and C
Pak choi	Beta-carotene, B vitamins, cancer-fighting phytochemicals, folic acid, vitamin C
Parsley	Calcium, iron, potassium, vitamins A and C
Parsnip	B vitamins, folic acid, inulin, potassium, vitamin E
Passion-fruit	Beta-carotene, phytochemicals which are antiseptic, sedative and mildly laxative, vitamin C
Pawpaw	Beta-carotene, flavonoids, magnesium, papain: a digestive enzyme, vitamin C
Peaches	Beta-carotene, flavonoids, potassium, vitamin C

ingredient	source of:
Peanuts	B vitamins, folic acid, protein, iron, zinc
Pears	Soluble fibre, vitamin C
Peppers	Beta-carotene, folic acid, potassium, phytochemicals that prevent blood clots, strokes and heart disease, vitamin C
Pineapple	Enzymes: especially bromelain, helpful for angina, arthritis and physical injury, vitamin C
Plums	Beta-carotene, malic acid: an effective aid to digestion, vitamins C and E
Pomegranate	Beta-carotene, enzymes with anti-diarrhoeal properties, heart-protective phytochemicals, vitamin E
Prunes	Beta-carotene, fibre, iron, niacin, potassium, vitamin B_6
Pumpkin	Folic acid, potassium, small amounts of B vitamins, vitamins A and C
Purslane	Essential fatty acids and cleansing bitter alkaloids, folic acid, vitamins C and E
Radishes	Iron, magnesium, phytochemicals that stimulate gall bladder and heal mucous membranes, potassium, vitamin C
Rosemary	Flavonoids, volatile oils: borneol, camphor, limonene
Sage	Phenolic acids, phyto-oestrogens, thujone: an antiseptic
Sauerkraut	Calcium, cancer-fighting phytochemicals, gut-protective lactic acid, potassium, vitamin C
Seaweed	Beta-carotene, calcium, iodine, iron, protein, magnesium, potassium, soluble fibre, vitamin $B_{12,}$ zinc
Sesame seeds	B vitamins, calcium, folic acid, magnesium, niacin, protein, vitamin E
Sorrel	Carotenoids, iron, protective phytochemicals, vitamin C

ingredient	source of:
Soya milk	Calcium, phytoestrogens especially genistein: a powerful breast, ovarian and prostate cancer-fighter, protein. If fortied, also vitamin D
Spinach	Beta-carotene, cancer-fighting phytochemicals, chlorophyll, folic acid, iron, lutein, xeaxanthine
Spring greens	Beta-carotene, cancer-fighting phytochemicals, carotenoids, iron, vitamin C
Spring onion	Cancer-fighting phytochemicals, diuretic, anti-arthritic and anti-inflammatory substances, folic acid, potassium, vitamins A and C
Stinging nettle	Beta-carotene, calcium, iron, vitamin C
Strawberries	Anti-arthritic phytochemicals, beta-carotene, vitamins C and E
Sweet potato	Beta-carotene and other carotenoids, cancer-fighting phytochemicals, protein, vitamins C and E
Tahini	B vitamins, calcium, folic acid, magnesium, niacin, protein, vitamin E
Thyme	Flavonoids, volatile oils: antiseptic thymol and carvol
Tomatoes	Beta-carotene, lycopene, potassium, vitamins C and E
Watercress	Anti-bacterial mustard oils, beta-carotene, iron, phenethyl isothiocyanate: specific lung cancer fighter for smokers, vitamins C and E
Watermelon	Folic acid, potassium, small amounts of B vitamins, vitamins A and C
Wheat germ	B vitamins, folic acid, iron, magnesium, potassium, vitamin E
Yoghurt: milk	Beneficial bacteria, calcium, protein, riboflavin, zinc
Yoghurt: soya	calcium, phytoestrogens, especially genistein: a powerful breast, ovarian and prostate cancer fighter. If fortified, also contains vitamin D

vitamins and minerals a-z

There's no doubt that vitamin and mineral supplements have a valuable role
to play both in the prevention and treatment of a wide variety of health
problems. However, what you get from a pill is something that has been artificially
manufactured – often with a higher potency than is necessary for good health.
In addition, the latest supplements are only what the scientists currently know about,
and history warns us that there must be many nutrients waiting to be discovered.
There is also a growing amount of evidence that naturally derived vitamins are
more effective than those which are synthetically manufactured, since they are
purer in origin and, in many cases, more easily absorbed by the body. Based on
that information, then, the safest course of action to take for a healthy lifestyle is
to ensure that you get an adequate supply of all essential nutrients from your food.
The best way to do that, of course, is through the regular consumption of your
own freshly produced Superjuices.

The following tables show which vitamins and minerals you need for good health,
what they do, and where to get them.

vitamins	essential for:	best food sources
A	Growth, skin, colour and night vision, immunity	Butter, cheese, chicken liver, cod liver oil, eggs, herring, lambs' liver, mackerel, salmon
B_1 (Thiamine)	Conversion of starchy foods into energy	Brewer's yeast (dried), peanuts, peanut butter, pork and pork products, sunflower seeds, vegetarian burger mixes, wheat germ, yeast extracts
B_2 (Riboflavin)	Converting fats and proteins into energy, also for mucous membranes and skin	Brewer's yeast, cheese, eggs, green leafy vegetables, liver, meat, soya products, wheat germ, yeast extracts, yoghurt
B_3 (Niacin)	Brain and nerve function, healthy skin, tongue and digestive organs.	Brewer's yeast (dried), cheese, dried fruits, eggs, nuts, oily fish, pigs' liver, poultry, wholegrain cereals, yeast extracts
B_6 (Pyridoxine)	Protein conversion, protection against heart disease, regulation of menstrual cycle, growth, nervous and immune systems	Bananas, beef, brewer's yeast, cod, herring, lentils, poultry, salmon, walnuts, wheat germ
B_{12}	Metabolism, nervous system, prevention of pernicious anaemia, proper formation of blood cells. With B_6, controls levels of homocysteine, which may cause heart disease	Beef, cheese, eggs, lamb, liver, oily fish, pork, seaweed

vitamins	essential for:	best food sources
Beta-carotene	Essential in its own right for protection against heart disease, cancer, and as an immune-booster. Not a vitamin in its own right, but listed here as it is also converted by the body into vitamin A (*see* above)	Apricots, chard, dark green and red leaf lettuce, dark leafy greens, mangoes, old carrots, pumpkin, red and yellow peppers, spinach, squashes, sweet potatoes, tomatoes, watercress, yellow melons
C	Natural immunity, wound healing, iron absorption, extremely powerful antioxidant that protects against heart disease, circulatory problems and cancers	All citrus fruits, all green vegetables, berries, currants, lettuces, peppers, potatoes, tomatoes, tropical fruits: guavas, mangoes, kiwi fruits and pineapple
D	Bone formation, protection from osteoporosis and rickets	Canned sardines, cod liver oil, eggs, fresh tuna, herring, kipper, mackerel, salmon, trout
E	Antioxidant protection of the heart and blood vessels, skin, immune-boosting and cancer-fighting	avocado, broccoli, nuts and seeds, peanut butter, safflower/sunflower/olive and other seed oils, spinach, sweet potatoes, watercress, wheat germ
Folic acid	Blood cells, prevention of birth defects, protects against anaemia	Brewer's yeast (dried), citrus fruits, eggs, dried fruits, fresh nuts, green leafy vegetables, liver, oats, pulses, soya flour, wheat germ

minerals	essential for:	best food sources
Calcium	Bone formation and prevention of osteoporosis, proper functioning of heart muscles and nerves	Brazil nuts, cheese, chickpeas, dried seaweeds, figs, greens, milk, shellfish, tinned sardines, tofu, whitebait, yoghurt
Iodine	Normal functioning of the thyroid gland	Cod, cockles, haddock (fresh or smoked), milk, mussels, seaweed, smoked mackerel, whelks
Iron	Red blood cells	Liver, kidney, dried apricots, wholemeal bread, spinach, raisins, prunes, dates, lentils, sesame and pumpkin seeds, legumes, nuts, dark-green leafy vegetables, beef and other meats
Magnesium	Energy-producing processes, the functions of vitamins B_1 and B_6, growth and repair	Almonds, Brazil nuts, brown rice, cashews, peas, pine nuts, sunflower and sesame seeds, soya-based protein, soya beans
Potassium	Normal cell function, nerves, control of blood pressure	Bananas, cheese, dried fruits, eggs, molasses, nuts, fresh fruit, fruit juices, raw vegetables, tea, wholemeal bread
Selenium	Powerful antioxidant: protects against heart disease, prostate cancer and lung cancer	Brazil nuts, dried mushrooms, lambs' kidneys and liver, lentils, sardines, sunflower seeds, tuna, walnuts, white fish, wholemeal bread
Zinc	Growth, hormone function, male fertility, liver function, immunity, taste	Cheese, dried seaweed, eggs, liver, oysters, pumpkin/sesame/sunflower seeds, pine nuts, shellfish, wholemeal bread

chemical robbery

Even in today's high-tech society, many doctors are unaware of the damaging effects some medicines, both prescriptive and over-the-counter, have on nutritional well-being. The fact is that the depletion of nutrients and other vital substances that results from long-term use of these 'chemical robbers' actually hinders the healing process. Chronic fatigue syndrome is a case in point: commonly caused by a zinc deficiency, it can also be a symptom of depression. If your doctor prescribes anti-depressants, they will, over time, interfere with zinc absorption – making you even more deficient in zinc and consequently more exhausted and depressed. The following is a list of common drug categories and their long-term effects on nutritional needs. When taking any for an extended period of time, give your body a boost with the relevant Superjuices in order to counteract or at least balance their thieving effects.

drug category	effect
Antacids	Increase the need for vitamins A, B complex, calcium, magnesium, iron and phosphorus
Antibiotics	Increase the need for B-complex vitamins because they destroy natural bacteria in the gut. Always eat live yoghurt every day when taking antibiotics
Anti-coagulants	Including warfarin; aspirin and all their relatives affect vitamin K
Anti-convulsants	Interfere with the body's absorption of vitamins B_6, D and K as well as folic acid. These drugs are normally taken for extended periods of time as in the treatment of epilepsy. Phenytoin (also used to treat irregular heartbeats) interferes with the absorption of calcium
Anti-inflammatory drugs	Sulfasalazine, which is prescribed for inflammatory bowel disease, causes a loss of folic acid. Rather than taking a supplement, it's much better to get your folic acid from a varied diet and fresh juices

drug category	effect
Anti-malarial drugs	Can also act against folic acid, and long-term use of may cause problems, such as anaemia and vision and hearing disturbances
Anti-ulcer drugs	Reduce the stomach's production of acid and can cause poor absorption of vitamin B_{12}
Cholesterol-lowering drugs	Increase the need for iron, beta-carotene, vitamins A, D, K, and folic acid
Diuretics	Many of these drugs deprive the body of B-complex vitamins potassium, magnesium and zinc
Drugs for high blood pressure	Hydralazine lowers the level of vitamin B_6 in the body
Laxatives	Laxatives cause a considerable loss of vitamins and minerals, especially calcium, phosphorous and vitamin D. This vitamin can be severely affected by long-term use, and its depletion puts women at a greater risk of osteoporosis, since vitamin D is essential for the efficient absorption of calcium
Oral contraceptives	The Pill is a major factor in nutritional status. It adversely affects folic acid, vitamins C and E, and B-complex vitamins
Sleeping pills and anti-depressants	Barbiturate-type sleeping pills affect the uptake of vitamin D. Anti-depressants interfere with the chemical process of B_2 absorption as well as with the absorption of the minerals zinc and magnesium
Tranquillizers	Stelazine is detrimental to vitamin B_{12} absorption

drink yourself better

condition	superjuice	effect	dose
Acne	Instant Energiser, p14	Skin-healing and cleansing	4 glasses a week
AMD	Eye Brite, p98	Highly protective carotenoids	2 glasses a week
Anaemia	Super Stinger, p77	Rich in iron and vitamin C	1 glass daily for 2 weeks, then 1 a week
Anxiety	Mediterranean Muscle, p25 Mock Mint Choc, p125	Soothing basil and honey and lots of B vitamins for nerves	As required
Arthritis	Ginger Spice, p38 Wake-up Whammy, p86	Anti-inflammatory, pain relieving and energising	At least 4 glasses a week
Asthma	Quartet in C, p41	Nourishes lung tissue, protects against infection	1 glass daily
Back pain	Pawpaw Punch, p55 Bunnies Bonanza, p72	Anti-inflammatory, diuretic, analgesic	1 glass daily, alternate between recipes
Blood sugar problems	Savoir Vivre, p100	Instant and slow-release energy to balance sugar levels	1 glass daily
Boils	Primary Pepper Juice, p18	Boosts resistance and detoxifying	1 glass daily if boils present, twice weekly as a preventative
Bronchitis	Doctor Garlic, p101	Antibacterial, immune boosting and expectorant	2 glasses daily during infection
Bruising	Oriental Magic, p64	Bromelain reduces bruising	1 glass daily as required

condition	superjuice	effect	dose
Catarrh	Horse Power, p21	Decongestant, mucous-membrane protector	1 glass daily when needed, 2 glasses a week as preventative
Chilblains	Soy Salsa, p96	Stimulates circulation, dilates peripheral blood vessels	2-3 glasses a week during winter
Cholesterol	The Guardian, p122 Dracula's Delight p92	Reduces cholesterol, protects against clotting and a little alcohol stimulates the circulation	At least 3 glasses a week of Dracula; not more than 2 with vodka
Chronic fatigue	Body-Builder, p126 Apple and Watercress Energiser, p44	Instant and slow-release energy boosts vitality	1 glass of one or the other recipe daily
Circulation problems	Hot and Juicy, p65	Dilates blood vessels, lowers cholesterol, stimulates circulation	1 glass on alternate days
Colds	C-Plus, p76	Provides a huge dose of immune-boosting vitamin C, bioflavonoids and echinacea	2 glasses a day throughout cold, and for 2 days afterwards
Constipation	Prune-light Express, p31	Provides masses of gently laxative soluble fibre	1 glass at bedtime
Cough	Doctor Garlic, p101	Antibacterial and expectorant, Immune-boosting	1 glass daily until better
Cramp	Buzz Juice, p87 Welsh Ginger, p81	Circulatory stimulant in ginger and extra potassium from banana are both cramp-preventative	1 glass of either in the evening for night cramp, or before sport (if cramp is exercise-induced)
Cystitis	Pink Punch, p107 (without vodka)	Antibacterial, specifically protects against bugs that cause cystitis	1 glass daily during infection, at least 3 glasses a week for prevention

condition	superjuice	effect	dose
Depression	Skinny Dip, p127 Scarborough Fair, p54	Provides lots of B vitamins and mentally-reviving aromatic oils	1 glass of either, daily
Dermatitis	Spring Clean Tonic, p58	Provides masses of vitamins A and C to stimulate skin-healing	3 glasses a week
Diarrhoea	Sweet Surrender, p63	Fluid replacement. Also harbours natural beneficial bacteria and anti-diarrhoeal properties	1 or 2 glasses daily as required
Diverticulitis	Long-life Lemonade, p90	Provides soluble fibre, healing vitamin A and lots of probiotic bacteria for healthy bowel function	1 glass every other day during acute episodes, twice a week for prevention
Eczema	Passionate Pumpkin, p70	Provides huge amount of skin-healing vitamins A and E	1 glass daily until clear
Fever	Paradiso, p119	Provides anti-inflammatory enzymes, anti-infective essential oils and lots of vitamin C	2 glasses a day until temperature falls
Fibrositis	Dandelion Delight, p29	Strongly diuretic. Eliminates pain-causing uric acid	2-3 glasses a week
Flatulence	The Florentine, p40	Provides soluble fibre for bowel function and anti-flatulence essential oils from fennel	Half a glass after meals
Fluid retention	Dandelion Delight, p29 Radish Revolution, p39	Both juices are strongly diuretic and rich in potassium for a balance of minerals	1 glass of either daily, when necessary
Fractures	Green Dream, p124	Provides lots of calcium and other minerals to speed bone healing	1 glass daily

condition	superjuice	effect	dose
Gallstones	Octet con Spirito, p59 Radish Revolution, p39	High in fibre to improve digestion. Garlic and radishes specifically stimulate gall bladder and liver function	1 glass of either daily
Gastritis	Lemon Express, p36	Antiseptic, antioxidant and soothing to the stomach lining For improved benefits, add 1 dessertspoon honey	2 glasses a day
Gingivitis	Good Mouthkeeping, p93	Antiseptic, antifungal and healing to the gums and mucous membranes of the mouth	1 glass daily, as long as necessary
Gout	Cucumber Soother, p91	Provides soothing enzymes, lots of vitamin A, anti-inflammatory and specific uric acid-reducing properties	1 glass daily during attacks, 2 glasses a week for prevention
Hair problems	Monkey Business, p116 Stir-fry Starter, p82	Contains minerals essential for good hair growth, including iodine, lots of vitamins C and E, and iron	Alternate these juices daily
Halitosis	Oriental Magic, p64	Antibacterial. Also provides healing enzymes and breath-freshening essential oils	1 glass daily, as required
Hay fever	Blue Passion, p45	Provides masses of vitamin C and especially protective bioflavonoids. For extra protection, add a dessertspoon of locally produced honey	1 glass daily
Headache	Femme Fatale, p66	Provides essential fatty acids, vitamins C and E. Liver-cleansing radishes stimulate circulation and reduce frequency	1 glass daily until headaches recede, then twice a week

condition	superjuice	effect	dose
Heart disease	Doctor Garlic, p101 Wake-up Whammy, p86	Provides heart-protective lycopenes and beta-carotenes. Also reduces risk of clots, and is a diuretic and a circulatory stimulant	Alternate a glass of each daily
Heartburn	Lime-E Shake, p118	Is soothing, nourishing and provides gut-beneficial bacteria	1 glass as required
Hepatitis	Cherry Ripe, p68 Pro-Bonus 2, p95	Strawberries and cherries are effective liver cleansers. Pro-Bonus 2 overflows with liver-nourishing nutrients and phytochemicals	2 glasses of each weekly
Herpes	Rainbow Cocktail, p35	Provides antiviral vitamin C and bioflavonoids	1 glass daily during attacks, 2 glasses weekly for protection
Hypertension	Doctor Garlic, p101 High Flyer, p15	Provides artery-protective phytochemicals and specific blood pressure-lowering properties	1 glass of either daily
Impotence	Spiced Silk, p120	Rich in vitamin E, zinc and selenium for improved function	2 or 3 glasses a week
Indigestion	Lime-E Shake, p118	Soothing, nourishing and provides gut-beneficial bacteria	1 glass as required
Infections	Pro-Bonus 1, p94 Back to School, p99	Provide an enormous boost to the natural immune system. Both juices are rich in natural anti-bacterials	1 glass of either daily during illness. At least 2 glasses a week for protection
Infertility	Femme Fatale, p66 Passionate Pumpkin, p70	Provides essential vitamin E, beta-carotenes and minerals for optimum fertility	1 glass of either daily

condition	superjuice	effect	dose
Influenza	Tropical Revitaliser, p47	Provides soothing enzymes for aches and pains, masses of vitamin C, beta-carotene for resistance and bioflavonoids for protection	1 or 2 glasses daily until you recover
Insomnia	Life Saver, p79	Provides natural sleep-inducing substances in lettuce, together with vitamin C and aromatic oils	1 glass before bed
Joint Pain	Ginger Spice, p38 Wake-up Whammy, p86	Anti-inflammatory, pain relieving and energising	At least 4 glasses a week
Kidney problems	Waterfall, p30 Pink Punch p107 (without vodka)	Diuretic and antiseptic	1 glass of either daily
Laryngitis	Welsh Ginger, p81 Scarborough Fair, p54	Provides volatile oils which are soothing and antiseptic, as well as the specific voice benefits of leeks.	1 glass of either daily, until better. Professional vocalists should drink Welsh Ginger twice a week for protection
Menstrual problems	Femme Fatale, p66 Spice Island Special, p121	Essential fatty acids in purslane,lots of vitamin E, and phytoestrogens in soya milk all help regulate the cycle	1 glass of either daily
Motion and early morning sickness	Ginger Spice, p38 Ginger Up Juice, p62	Volatile oils in ginger prevent sickness	1 glass of either before travelling or as required
Mouth ulcers	Melon and Mango Tango, p22 Good Mouthkeeping, p93	Rich in healing beta-carotenes and natural anti-bacterials and enzymes	1 glass as required. Take regularly for prevention
Obesity	Skinny Dip, p127 Agen Provocateur, p123	Full of nutrients, low in calories	1 glass as a replacement for one meal daily

condition	superjuice	effect	dose
Osteoporosis	Mock Mint Choc, p125 Soy Salsa, p96 Stir-fry Starter, p82	All contain calcium and other trace minerals, selenium, zinc and iron	1 glass of each daily, in rotation
PMS	Spice Island Special, p121 Mountain Rescue, p71	Provides phytoestrogens and essential oils, together with extra iron and enzymes. Also diuretic, so reduces bloating	Alternate 1 glass of each for 7 days before and during the the first 2 days of each period
Prostate problems	Watermelon Man, p34	Protective phytochemicals and masses of beta-carotene are prostate protectors. Drink with a handful of pumpkin seeds	1 glass daily until symptoms improve, then 3 times a week
Psoriasis	Passionate Pumpkin, p70	Provides huge amounts of skin healing vitamins A and E	1 glass daily
Raynaud's Syndrome (constricted circulation in the extremities)	Peppery Pick-up, p83 Calvados Cure-all, p113	Enormous quantities of beta-carotene improve the quality of blood vessels, while the ginger and alcohol in the Cure All dilate blood vessels and stimulate circulation	Alternate 1 glass of either daily during cold weather
Restless legs	Red-eye Special, p16	Provides iron, diuretics and carotenoids to calm this distressing problem	1 glass during the evening as required
Rheumatism	Ginger Spice, p38 Wake-up Whammy, p86	Anti-inflammatory, pain-relieving and energising	At least 4 glasses a week
Seasonal Affective Disorder (SAD)	Women's Wonder, p32 Pepper Purifier, p37	Provides B vitamins, vitamin A and iron. Both these juices provide essential nutrients that also help this condition	Alternate 1 glass of either, daily, during the winter

condition	superjuice	effect	dose
Shingles	Rainbow Citrus Cocktail, p35 Welsh Ginger, p81	Super-rich in antiviral vitamin C and bioflavonoids. Leeks and ginger can be helpful for residual pain	1 glass of either daily, as necessary
Sinusitis	Horse Power p21	Decongestant and mucous-membrane protective	Daily when needed, 2 glasses a week as preventative
Sore throat	Welsh Ginger p81 Scarborough Fair, p54	Provides volatile oils that are soothing and antiseptic; also vocal benefits of leeks	A glass of either daily. Vocalists should drink Welsh Ginger twice a week for protection
Stomach ulcers	Tutti-Frutti, p48	Provides healing bioflavonoids, vitamin C and enzymes. Will be enhanced by adding 1 dessertspoon of honey	1 glass daily
Thyroid problems	Stir-fry Starter, p82	Specially rich in iodine, other trace minerals and vitamin A	2 glasses a week
Tonsillitis	Tropical Revitaliser, p47	Full of protective anti-bacterial nutrients and especially throat-soothing enzymes	3 or 4 small glasses daily
Varicose veins	Quick, Quick, Sloe, p108 Pumping Iron, p19	Quick, Quick, Sloe provides enormous amounts of beta-carotene combined with sloe gin as an occasional circulatory tonic. Pumping Iron provides regular ongoing vascular support	Quick Quick Sloe: no more than twice a week. Pumping Iron: daily

detox juice diet

If you've over-indulged and feel a bit sluggish, it's time for the Superjuice Detox Plan. Boost immunity; ward off colds; cleanse your liver and colon; rest your kidneys... and as a bonus, lose four or five pounds.

There are few calories, here, so be warned: you'll feel hungry. But don't cheat; you'll thank yourself for it later. There's also no coffee and only weak tea, which means no caffeine, and that's almost certain to cause headaches. Avoid the pain killers, though, and drink masses of water. The headaches are transient, and you're going to feel great by day four and bursting with protective antioxidants.

I advise you to start the first two days of the diet when your workload is at its lightest.

day one

Breakfast Pro-Bonus 1 (page 94) One orange, half a grapefruit, one large slice of melon. Herb tea with honey

Lunch Pro-Bonus 2 (page 95) A plateful of raw red and yellow peppers, cucumber, tomato, broccoli, cauliflower, celery, carrots, radishes and lots of fresh parsley. Add extra-virgin olive oil and lemon juice as a dressing

Evening meal Peak Performer (page 17). Large mixed salad: lettuce, tomato, watercress, onion, garlic, beetroot, celeriac, fresh mint and any herbs you like. Add extra-virgin olive oil and lemon juice as a dressing

day two

Breakfast Paradiso (page 119). Hot water with a thick slice of lemon

Mid-morning Bunnies' Bonanza (page 72). A handful each of raisins, dried apricots and fresh nuts

Lunch Long-life Lemonade (page 90) A large salad of green leaves with radishes, celery, a sprinkle of sunflower seeds, lemon juice and olive oil. Herb or weak Indian tea with honey (no milk)

Mid-afternoon Lemon Express (page 36)

Evening meal Spring Clean Tonic (page 58) Large jacket potato drizzled with olive oil and black pepper. Herb tea or weak Indian tea

During the evening A mixture of dried fruits and unsalted nuts and as much fresh fruit as you like

day three

Breakfast Blue Passion (page 45). A carton of live yoghurt mixed with a tablespoon of unsweetened muesli. Weak tea or herb tea

Mid-morning Minty Morning (page 28). Six dried apricots.

Lunch Life Saver (page 79) A small bowl of raisins, sultanas, walnuts and almonds. Herb or weak Indian tea

Mid-afternoon Cherry Ripe (page 68)

Evening meal Waterfall (page 30). A bowl of pasta with chopped garlic, olive oil and fresh, chopped tomatoes. A large mixed salad A carton of low-fat live yoghurt. Herb or weak Indian tea

Treat your system gently on Day Four, and don't rush back to normal eating. Avoid red meat, and start with plainly cooked chicken or fish, some starchy foods, plenty of fruit, salads and vegetables. And no dairy products except yoghurt, by the way, until Day Five.

juicing: a practical guide

What and how to juice

The whole point of juicing is to get the maximum possible amount of vitamins, minerals, enzymes and all those amazing phytochemicals (plant substances) out of food and into your body. For this reason, buy organic produce whenever possible – especially if you're juicing for babies and small children. Make sure your produce is in peak condition, and don't be tempted to buy reduced-price leftovers from your local market late on Saturday. if you're a gardener, however, juicing is a great way to use the inevitable glut of produce that crops up around harvest time. Single juices such as apple, pear or tomato freeze extremely well; 'recycle' plastic milk containers for this purpose.

Wash all produce thoroughly, scrubbing tough-skinned varieties with a soft brush. All fruits and vegetables should be juiced with their skins, except where otherwise stated. Non-organic produce should be washed in a solution of one teaspoon of washing up liquid to a litre of warm water and then rinsed thoroughly; this removes most external chemical residues.

Don't prepare and chop up produce before you need it as this causes unnecessary vitamin loss. When juicing small quantities of ingredients – six mint leaves, a small piece of ginger, a few sage leaves – wrap them in one of the other ingredients first. When using ice, put it in the liquidiser with a little water and switch on for a few seconds before adding the other ingredients.

All the recipes are based on my own personal taste and experience, but once you get the hang of juicing, you'll want to experiment with your own concoctions. Don't worry if you're missing a specific ingredient: use your imagination and make an appropriate substitution. At the end of the day, there are no rules to juicing, and you'll soon find out what your family favourites are.

Choosing the ideal machine

The most versatile combination is to have a juice extractor and a liquidiser. You can get citrus attachments for most juicers – or, indeed, buy a separate one – but I think it's better to peel citrus fruits (leaving as much pith behind as possible, of course) and put them through a juicer. As with all things, you get what you pay for, and the more expensive machines will work out cheaper in the long run. They last longer, for one thing, and they extract more juice, so you get better value for your money. On the other hand, if you're a beginner and just want to dip your toe in the water, start with an inexpensive machine and see how you get on. I've used four machines to prepare all the recipes in this book:

The Kenwood Centrifugal Juicer at around £40 is universally available. This really is great value for money and separates the pulp from the juice quite efficiently. It's very easy to clean, the only drawback being the capacity of the pulp collector. For large quantities, you'll have to stop and empty the machine from time to time. Similar machines at around the same price are made by Braun and Moulinex.

The Waring Professional Liquidiser available from major department stores and kitchen shops, costs £149. This is the one you see in cocktail bars and juice bars; again, it's not the cheapest on the market, but it has a very powerful motor, a large capacity jug and two-speed operation. It's extremely easy to clean and will last a lifetime.

The Waring Professional Juicer made by the Dynamics Corporation of America, is available from major department stores and kitchen shops at around £239. This is a highly efficient centrifugal machine which produces a much drier pulp; consequently you get more juice. It's obviously built to last, and the bowl, cutters and lid are made of stainless steel. You'll make more juice before needing to empty the strainer basket but it's by no means the easiest machine to clean.

The Champion, made by Plastaket Mfg Co, California, is available from Wholistic Research Company, Cambridge at around £350. This is what's called a masticating juicer. It mashes fresh produce and squeezes the juices through a stainless-steel screen, extruding the pulp through a separate nozzle. Just tie a plastic bag on the end and you can juice all day. Yes, it's expensive, but it's guaranteed for five years and you can also use it for grinding up seeds, nuts, dried and frozen fruits. You can even make your own peanut butter in it!

If you've already tried your hand at juicing and can afford to spend this sort of money, it'll be a great investment in your health. Whatever juicer you choose, make sure you have a permanent place for it on your worktop, as it's a bit too heavy to get in and out of a cupboard every time you want to use it. In fact, my advice is always leave your juicer and blender accessible and ready to go: it's a great incentive to use them every day.

glossary

Age-related Macular Degeneration (AMD) Disease of the retina which results in gradual vision loss, particularly of the ability to focus on or recognise fine detail. The *macula lutea*, is the part of the retina that controls visual acuity.

Anthocyanidins/Anthocyanin Any of the soluble pigments that produce blue to red colouring in flowers and plants.

Antibiotic A substance produced by a micro-organism that is able to inhibit or kill another micro-organism.

Antioxidant A substance that inhibits oxidation. In the body, antioxidants are thought to prevent the destruction of vitamin C, slow the destruction of body cells and strengthen the immune system.

Beta-carotene A powerful antioxidant which the body transforms into vitamin A.

Betanin Substance that produces the red colouring in beetroot

Bile The yellowish-green fluid secreted by the liver that aids digestion and the absorption of fats.

Bioflavonoid Also known as vitamin P, a biologically active flavonoid.

Bromelain An enzyme obtained from pineapple juice.

Capsaicin A colourless irritant found in various capsicums, or peppers.

Carotene Any one of the orange and red pigments that occur in carrots and other plants as well as in egg yolks and butter which is converted into vitamin A.

Carotenoid Any one of the various (usually) yellow to red pigments found widely in plants and animals.

Chlorophyll The green colouring matter in plants.

Chronic Fatigue Syndrome Chronic lethargy or exhaustion that is usually lifestyle related.

Collagen The most abundant protein in the human body and a major structural component of many of its parts, including skin and tendons.

Coumarin A white lactone that beneficially affects blood flow.

Cystitis Inflammation of the bladder.

Diurectic Any substance that increases the production of urine by the kidneys.

Echinacea Native American herb that is beneficial to the immune system. Its anti-microbial properties make it effective in the prevention of colds and flu.

Ellagic acid A natural chemical substance found in some tannins.

Enzyme A chemical substance produced by living cells.

Expectorant Any substance that promotes discharge of mucus from the respiratory tract.

Fatty acid Any of the numerous beneficial fats that occur naturally in fats, waxes and essential oils and are, among other things, good for the heart.

Fenchone A phytochemical in fennel that stimulates the liver.

Flavone A beneficial phytochemical found in leaves, stems and seed capsules of some plants.

Flavonoid A beneficial phytochemical that tends to occur in plants which are high in vitamin C.

Folic acid A vitamin of the B complex used to treat nutritional anaemias.

Free radical Naturally occurring oxygen molecules that damage the body and are thought to play a significant role in the aging process.

Gingerol Volatile oil present in ginger which stimulates circulation.

Gout Metabolic disease marked by painful inflammation of the joints and an excess amount of uric acid in the blood.

Indole A volatile oil of the same family as gingerol (*see* above).

Inulin A tasteless, white substance found mainly in the roots and rhizomes of some plants.

Lactone A beneficial volatile oil.

Lecithin A complex fat found in egg yolks and Brazil nuts. Lecithin contains choline, a substance the body converts into acetylcholine, which is essential for the smooth flow of nerve impulses.

Limonene A substance that occurs in the essential oils of many citrus fruits.

Linoleic acid A liquid unsaturated fatty acid found in oils that is thought to be essential for nutrition.

Lutein A beneficial orange pigment occurring in plants.

Lycopene A carotenoid pigment that forms the colouring matter in tomatoes.

Myalgic Encephalomylitis (ME) A condition involving tiredness, muscle pain, lack of concentration, panic attacks, memory loss and depression that usually follows a viral infection.

Mucous membrane Any of the membranes rich in mucous glands that line body passages such as the nose.

Opiate Any substance that induces rest or quiets uneasiness.

Osteoporosis A disease involving the weakening of bone that is caused by a loss of calcium.

Papain An enzyme present in the juice of papayas that breaks down proteins.

Parkinson's Disease Progressive nervous disease marked by tremor, weakness of resting muscles and a peculiar gait.

Pectin Soluble fibre that adds bulk and soothes the gut. Apples are particularly rich in pectin.

Phytochemical Any of the natural chemicals that occur in plants.

Phytoestrogen Any of the oestrogen-like chemicals that naturally occur in plants.

Pinene A beneficial substance similar to limonene (*see* above) that is found mainly in tropical fruits.

Probiotic bacteria Beneficial bacteria.

Seasonal Affective Disorder (SAD) Disorder in which a person's moods change with the seasons, most pointedly showing depression in winter.

Salicylate Bitter-tasting substance found in plants (*eg* willow bark) that is used to reduce fever.

Sinigrin An antibiotic volatile oil found in horseradish that is particularly protective and stimulating to the mucous membranes.

Tannin Any of the soluble, astringent substances found in plants.

Terpene A substance found in essential oils, such as those present in conifers.

Thujone A volatile oil that is beneficial in small doses.

Toxin A poisonous substance produced by bacteria.

Uric acid A crystalline acid that occurs in the urine of most animals. Too much uric acid in the bloodstream can collect in the joints, causing intense pain.

Virus Any agent that causes an infectious disease.

Xeaxanthine A carotenoid that is of particular benefit to the eyes.

Zingiberene Beneficial volatile oil found in ginger that stimulates circulation.

index

Entries in **bold** are juice names.

m

magnesium 24-5, 30, 34, 44, 57, 68-9,
  80, 82-3, 94-5, 100, 108, 112, 116,
  118-19, 122, 141
mandarins 135
manganese 113
mango 22, 45, 47, 70, 87, 108, 117, 119, 135
mangosteen 87
ME 74-5, 82
medication, juices to follow 35, 37
mediterranean muscle 25
melon 16, 22, 34, 45, 55, 100
melon and mango tango 22
memory, improving 15, 54, 123
menopause 32, 95
menstrual cycle 29, 32, 70, 85, 149
mental stimulation 15, 54, 80, 123
migraine 50
milk 117-18, 124, 126, 135
mint 16, 24, 28, 96, 110, 115, 125, 135
minty morning 28
mock mint choc 125
molasses 83, 123, 126, 135
monkey business 116
mooli 101, 135
morning sickness 119, 149
mountain rescue 71
mouth care 91, 93
mucous membranes 58, 90-1, 144
muscles, tired 25

n

night vision 14, 98
nutmeg 115, 124, 135
nuts 61, 88, 126

o

octet con spirito 59
on your mark 84
opiates 69
oranges 28, 35, 38, 76, 78-9, 83,
  108-9, 118, 135
oriental magic 64
osteoporosis 32, 94-5, 149

p

pain-killer 53
pak choi 82, 135
papain 55
papaya 111
paradiso 119
Parkinson's disease 43
parsley 14, 16, 20, 24, 30, 37, 54, 72,
  81, 98, 105, 127, 135
parsnip 84, 135
passion-fruit 45, 48, 87, 117, 135
passionate pumpkin 70
pawpaw 55, 67, 136
pawpaw punch 55
peaches 48, 53, 108, 136
peak performer 17
peanut butter 116, 136
pears 17, 31, 33, 40, 46, 52-3, 85, 123, 136
pectin 17, 31, 33, 40, 46, 49, 104, 110, 116
pepper purifier 37
peppers 18, 37, 58, 83, 95, 136
peppery pick-up 83
phosphorus 59, 73, 83-4, 94, 110,
  119, 122
phytochemicals 46, 52, 57, 64, 72,
  81-2, 85, 89, 92, 96, 107, 120
phytoestrogens 32, 66, 72
pick-me-up juices 74-87
pineapple 17, 47, 64, 91, 99, 111,
  119, 136
pinene 120
pink punch 107
plums 49, 136
PMS 29, 32, 149
pollutants 18, 26, 47
pomegranate 48, 136
potassium 14-18, 20-1, 24-5, 28, 30, 32,
  34-7, 39-41, 44-6, 49, 51-7, 59, 63-5,
  68-9, 71, 73, 77-84, 86-7, 90-7, 99-100,
  104-5, 107-8, 110, 112, 116-18, 122-3,
  125-7, 141
power pack 46
pregnancy 19, 30, 119
primary pepper punch 18
pro-bonus 1 94
pro-bonus 2 95
proanthocyanidins 51
probiotic bacteria 35
protein 73, 85, 116, 120-1,
  124-5, 127
prune-light express 31
prunes 31, 123, 136
pumping iron 19
pumpkin 65, 70, 136
purslane 66, 136

q

quartet in 'C' 41
quick, quick, sloe 108

r

radish revolution 39
radishes 39, 59, 66, 90, 93, 101,
  104, 136
rain forest freezer 111
rainbow cocktail 35
ready, steady, go 85
red-eye special 16
rheumatism 68, 112,
  123, 150
rosemary 54, 61, 136
rum, white 106

s

SAD *see* Seasonal Affective Disorder
saffron 70
sage 54, 91, 136
salad leaves 69, 135
salicylates 53
saliva glands, stimulation 27-8, 93
satsumas 135
sauerkraut 90, 136
savoir vivre 100
scarborough fair 54
Seasonal Affective Disorder 74, 150
seaweed 82, 136
sedative 79
seeds 61
selenium 39, 61, 125, 131, 141
sesame seeds 70, 82, 120, 137
shakes 114-27
silica 97
silicon 69, 84
sinigrin 21
sinuses 90-1, 150
skin 14, 26-7, 41, 51, 58, 97, 105,
  108, 112, 124
  ageing 15
  sun damage 15
skin deep 97
skinny dip 127
sloe gin 108
smoothies 114-27
sorrel 24, 137
soy salsa 96

author's note

My thanks are due to Mitchell Beazley, and particularly to my commissioning editor, Margaret Little, who waged a titanic struggle against great odds and the demands of my many commitments. Thankfully, her combined use of sticks and carrots – essential for a juicing book! – got the manuscript finished. Editor Jamie Ambrose worked tirelessly, uncomplainingly and always with a sense of humour through the entire text. And, as always, my desperately overworked secretary Janet burnt lots of midnight oil and drank far too many cups of midnight coffee to help me write this book.

Without all of them, it would never have seen the light of day.

Michael van Straten